14

D0462308

French Grand Opera

AN *Art* AND A *Business*

French Grand Opera

AN ART AND A BUSINESS

SUBMITTED IN PARTIAL FULFILLMENT OF THE
REQUIREMENTS FOR THE DEGREE OF DOCTOR
OF PHILOSOPHY, IN THE FACULTY OF PHILOSOPHY,
COLUMBIA UNIVERSITY

BY WILLIAM LORAN CROSTEN

PUBLISHED BY KING'S CROWN PRESS

COLUMBIA UNIVERSITY

NEW YORK, 1948

To Mary

PREFACE

I N the entire history of the lyric stage there is hardly a parallel to the fabulous success enjoyed by Meyerbeer and his associates at the Paris Opéra beginning in 1831. Carrying all before them, they created a type of lyric drama which not only won a local triumph but left its mark wherever opera was played. There was opposition, but it proved fruitless. Former favorites were shunted aside and even Wagner, himself, was unable to halt the conquest.

At least from an historical point of view, therefore, French grand opera of the 1830's cannot be disregarded or dismissed with a phrase. Its one-time glory is now woefully faded, but its place in nineteenth-century annals is important. In the commercial world it is outstanding for its shrewd analysis of the theatrical market; as an art form it is notable for its attempt to give a new, large-scale design to opera; and as a social document it provides numerous clues to an understanding of the era in France following the Revolution of 1830. Considering all these things, it would appear, then, that there is room for a more comprehensive study of this style of musical theater than has heretofore been available.

In the preparation of this book I naturally incurred several obligations which I am happy to acknowledge. The *Musical Quarterly* (G. Schirmer, Inc.) kindly allowed me to quote from articles by myself and others which appeared in that journal; the Librairie Académique Perrin, Paris, granted me the use of material from *Les Années romantiques de Balzac* by Louis J. Arrigon; and I am indebted to Routledge & Kegan Paul Ltd., London, for permission to quote from Wagner's *Prose Works*. Thanks are due also to Abram Loft for many favors. Finally, I should like to record my gratitude to Professors Douglas Moore, Paul H. Láng, Jacques Barzun, Jean-Albert Bédé, and Milton Smith of Columbia University, whose advice was invaluable and whose friendly encouragement was a constant support.

W. L. C.

TABLE OF CONTENTS

I

GRAND OPERA: A UNION OF ART AND BUSINESS

GRAND OPERA is employed today both as a pseudo-classification and as an expression of disparagement. In either case it is used incorrectly. On the one hand the term is loosely taken to include practically anything from Bach's *Phoebus and Pan* to Wagner's *Die Götterdämmerung*, as long as the work is deemed worthy by our theater managers of presentation at a major opera house. Far more serious, however, is the pernicious misuse of "grand opera" by some critics to specify a branch of the musical theater which is presumed to be a sort of commodious catch-all exclusively devoted to the glorification of pure spectacle.

The confusion in nomenclature comes from substituting "grand opera" for the single word "opera" which in France has been a general designation for serious lyric drama ever since the opening of the Académie Royale de Musique in 1671. The phrase "grand opera" began to be used extensively only in the nineteenth century, and it will clarify matters to limit its application to the particular kind of lyric theater with which it was chiefly associated: namely to that which arose in Paris during the late 1820's and which received final definition in 1836 with the production of Giacomo Meyerbeer's *Les Huguenots*. Lully (1632–1687), in recognition of the strong literary basis of his work, called it *tragédie lyrique*. Gluck (1714–1787) likewise publicized his intentions in *Alceste* (1767) by including in the title the words *tragedia per musica*.

Meyerbeer (1791–1864) gave no such descriptive label to his pieces, but it is to them that the name "grand opera" specifically applies. It is also to what is often barely a casual acquaintance with his works that we can trace most of the current half-truths which cloud our conception of the grand opera style.

While Meyerbeer, however, is usually regarded as the symbol of French grand opera, he was by no means its sole creator. The establishment of this type of theater, in fact, was not so much the work of any one man as the result of the unique collaboration of several, including Meyerbeer the composer, Scribe the librettist, Duponchel and Cicéri the scene designers, and Véron the director of the Opéra. The role of the composer in the emergence of grand opera is equal but hardly superior to that of either the dramatist or the *metteurs en scène*. The latter brought with them the spectacular new tableaux developed in the optical entertainments of the popular theaters after 1800. Scribe, master of *vaudeville* and the well-made play, turned his skill to the problem of animating the vast revolutionary décors he found available at the opera house. And Meyerbeer set himself to writing scores which would make possible a successful fusion of spectacle, action, and music. Binding all of these men and their efforts together is the somewhat gaudy figure of Véron, whose ideas permeated every corner of the opera house and under whose brilliant directorship the Académie became the showplace of Europe.

If Meyerbeer is not wholly responsible for the birth of grand opera, neither was music the first of its elements to receive definition. Indeed, the distinctive grand opera score was somewhat tardy in making its appearance. The pictorial and dramatic bases of the structure were laid by Cicéri and Scribe as early as 1828 in *La Muette de Portici;* but music lacked a conclusive model until Meyerbeer's *Robert le Diable* was played in 1831.

This sequence of events indicates that at the root of grand opera lies a scenic development going hand in hand with the invasion of France's first theaters by popular dramatic techniques and materials. It also shows that the strength of this opera is not contained merely in the exploitation of a single feature. *La Muette de Portici* was a spectacular demonstration of the scene painter's art, but it did not establish a course in theatrical history. The ascendancy of the new style waited upon the more perfect blending of elements which took place in *Robert le Diable*. Bringing together for the first time the chief architects of grand opera, this decisive work certified beyond doubt that a new epoch had arrived, and by so doing it became the piece which set the tone in the French lyric theater for the rest of the nineteenth century. The union of talents was not founded at one stroke, but it was only after all the principals had joined forces that grand opera emerged as a full-grown style able to win its way in the competition of the theater.

It can hardly be overemphasized that French opera of the 1830's displays a real union, not a senseless mélange of arts. It shows what Paul H. Láng calls the romantic urge to "seize upon and unify everything." [1] More particularly, it is the closest approach in its day to the ideal synthesis of arts dreamed of by many and invoked by Alfred de Vigny in his poem *La Beauté idéale, aux mânes de Girodet* (1825).

> Descends donc, triple lyre, instrument inconnu,
> O toi! qui parmi nous n'es pas encore venu
> Et qu'en se consumant invoque le génie,
> Sans toi point de beauté, sans toi point d'harmonie;
> Musique, poésie, art pur de Raphaël
> Vous deviendrez un Dieu . . . mais sur un seul autel!

In other respects, too, grand opera accepted the lead of Romanticism. Seeking unity, it exhibited a democratic and often bewildering variety of characteristics. The opera recognized and followed the "Gothic" trend in literature toward the fantastic and the supernatural. At the same time it showed its awareness of the current interest in the study of history and in questions of social welfare by turning its attention to subject matter of an historical nature which might be related to contemporary issues. It did not pretend to serve as a forum of public opinion, but was far from indifferent to the problems of the day. Opera joined the literary and graphic arts in their pursuit of local color, in their care for exactitude of detail in costume and scene. One sees likewise that the same impulse which led the romantic poets toward a more definite, picturesque language impelled Meyerbeer to extend greatly the color and expressive range of the opera orchestra.

In all these things grand opera is truly "romantic." This, however, is only one side of the picture. The other side shows the entry of the commercial element. At that point the opera becomes a work of compromise engineered by men who understood the main tenets of Romanticism and were able to judge with some accuracy to what extent that movement was acceptable to the theater public. Grand opera is thus more than a union of arts. It is also a marriage between business and art, and as such is an outstanding example of bourgeois commercial expansion during the early years in the reign of Louis-Philippe (1830–1848).

"Sometime ago," says a character in Scribe's play *Le Mariage d'Argent* (1827), "the fine arts revolted and decided no longer to allow themselves to die of hunger." [2] Despite this sensible resolution, occasional artists no doubt still were being underfed; but it is evident that those associated with the Opéra after 1831 were among the ones least likely to suffer from malnutrition. Their lot was more secure because grand opera became the greatest public success in the history of the French lyric stage. There have been other alliances between business and art but none more brilliant than that which existed at the Paris Opéra in the 1830's under the aegis of Doctor Véron.

This self-styled "bourgeois of Paris," [3] who spoke and acted as if he had stepped out of a play by Scribe, asked only one thing of opera: that it render a profit. Theoretical problems of aesthetics consequently were of less concern to him than to some of his predecessors. The ideas and the ideals which animated Lully in the early years of French opera or which led Gluck to his later Parisian works were no longer primary. Any theory of opera, be it old or new, romantic or otherwise, gained the interest of Véron only after it was strained through the policies of the highly organized business concern called the Académie Royale de Musique. And while this did not necessarily preclude everything of a high artistic nature, it did mean that grand opera from the start was subject to certain definite and inflexible trade considerations.

Véron knew his public. He knew how restricted was the actual circle dominated by Romanticism; and he realized that the majority of his audience would be composed either of those who looked to opera for light diversion—the pastiche and pot-pourri fanciers—or of those who played with the trappings of Romanticism and liked to imagine themselves touched by that movement because to do so was à la mode. For such a public, recruited in large part from the business and professional classes which rose to positions of power after the July Revolution of 1830, a special kind of musical theater was necessary. Véron and his associates judged that a blend of romantic and conventional elements would be more saleable by far than any purer product of Romanticism. On that estimate they gambled their talents and money, and it is no exaggeration to say that neither before nor since have producers of opera ever gauged their audience's capacity with greater nicety. Hollywood, using a different medium but with ideas and standards of effect often remarkably similar to those of grand opera, furnishes our only contemporary parallel.

The opera's authors were not only shrewd judges of public taste, but were themselves peculiarly fitted by temperament and experience to satisfy that demand. Véron, the incarnation of bourgeois sensibilities, fortunately found in Scribe and Meyerbeer the creative talents to which his own managerial ability made the perfect complement. Both artists were skilled craftsmen and neither came to the Opéra bound by party affiliations or weighted with any doctrinaire enthusiasm. They were alert to Romanticism, but remained independent enough to adopt its program only so far as their purposes required. Scribe had worked his way up through the popular *vaudeville* and knew from his experience as France's favorite playwright what was necessary in his day to get and to keep an audience. Meyerbeer, seeking his true métier after early studies in Germany and subsequent essays in Italian opera, found his proper niche in the more international Parisian grand opera and brought to it an equipment sufficiently eclectic to suit almost any segment of opinion. To such men as these there was neither an intellectual hardship nor any great mechanical difficulty involved in cutting their work to the size of the Opéra and its public.

Grand opera then is an extremely practical sort of art in which expediency often seems to be raised to a principle. It is an art compounded of the familiar and the novel, of convention and originality. On the surface at least it is a compilatory form. Gioachino Rossini (1792–1868) furnished Meyerbeer his model of vocalism, Johann Simon Mayr (1763–1845) and Giovanni Pacini (1796–1867) paved the way for his orchestral expansion, and Gasparo Spontini (1774–1851) gave him examples of massed choral writing. To the more romantic elements of subject and setting were added the vivid action and moralistic tone of the popular melodrama, and the luxury of scene traditional with French opera ever since the baroque era.

Obviously, grand opera includes a great many things. Its authors unhesitatingly took whatever they wanted from any available source; but what is more important, they never failed to select the materials and methods best suited to their expressive aims. Also, they never fell into the error of thinking that a collection of odds and ends makes an opera. There is as little miscalculation of effect in their works as there is confusion of direction. The great diversity of spectacle and music is assuredly one part of the picture—perhaps the most important aspect to the contemporary public. It should not blind us, however, to the presence of a much more interesting and unique feature: the formal organization of whole scenes into large-scale musico-dramatic patterns. These are worked out so consistently and methodically that they leave no doubt of the intention to create in grand opera a unity of sight and sound far broader in scope than anything previously attempted.

The few men jointly responsible for its design accomplished their aim in the short period of years from 1831 to 1836; and although their personalities differed, they displayed such singleness of purpose with respect to opera that generalizations become possible. Bearing this in mind, we find ample warrant for thinking of grand opera as a genuine style, not a notion counter. We are no less justified in holding it up as a valid approach from the standpoint of the French theater to the formal problems explored in Wagner's *Gesamtkunstwerk*. The two conceptions of the lyric stage are often violently opposed, but in more ways than one, Wagner is indebted to the example of grand opera. That complex and much-maligned theatrical form thus bowed to the present and cast its shadow into the future.

Although built to the specifications of its home public, it reached far beyond the city of Paris in its effect.[4] As an art or as a business its position in the nineteenth century is significant. Indeed, it is of such importance that its clarification becomes not only an interesting task but a possible contribution to a better understanding of both operatic and literary history of the romantic period.

II

THE ADMINISTRATION OF
THE OPERA

A S A BUSINESS, the Opéra of the 1830's shared the point of view and the methods of the large commercial houses of the day. And like them, it gained much of its character from the fact that the controlling voice in society now came from the bourgeois level.

For many years, and particularly since the fall of Napoleon, it was evident that the economic power in France was gradually coming to rest in the hands of the bourgeoisie. Their influence increased as the restrictions on their business activities diminished. The expansion of commerce had been strictly curtailed by the older mercantilist regulations and the many local trade barriers, but as these were scrapped a new system of free industrial competition was instituted. With it began the modern domination of all classes by the business world. Industry did not yet have the habit of great enterprises and could not have it until the development of the railroad; but by 1820, thanks to the stabilizing of public credit and the capable handling of public finances under Louis XVIII, private capital was becoming much less timid. Business men ventured successfully into all branches of commerce and industry, and as their operations were extended and their accumulations increased the conviction grew in them that "they were the important figures in society and that the state should be run for their benefit." [1]

From 1815 to 1820 it appeared reasonable to think that their ambitions might be reconciled with the existing Bourbon government. The assassination, however, of the Duc de Berri in 1820 and the subsequent release of all the repressed hatred of the ultra-royalists for any stripe of economic or political liberalism made a compromise increasingly difficult. The wounds of the Revolution were again opened, and Louis' tyrannical successor, Charles X, seemed determined to aggravate them. "The first Revolution [1789] while wishing to effect a mingling of classes and hierarchies only succeeded in separating them more distinctly. It resulted not in fusion but in war. The aristocrats went into exile and returned with their same grand airs. Napoleon, moreover, did not require them to yield obeisance. Naturally the Restoration consolidated them in their pride." [2] Despite the bourgeois desire to avoid violence, liberals were finally left no alternative to actual revolt. The event was precipitated by the publication of the five Royal Ordinances of July 25, 1830, and within two days the people of Paris had taken up arms against the king.

Barricades once more blocked the Parisian streets. This time, though, the struggle was short and relatively little damage was done the city. "Three glorious days" of revolution, July 27–29, were enough to force the intransigent Charles to flee across the Channel again to England and to put an end to the long line of Bourbon monarchs in France; but they did not bring in their wake a united or a satisfied nation. As people soon discovered, the triumph of the insurgents merely created a favorable opportunity for the upper bourgeoisie to make themselves the political as well as the economic masters of the country.

Toward the end of Charles' bitterly reactionary career the differing voices of the opposition had merged into one great unison cry of defiance. Republicans, Bonapartists, and liberal Constitutionalists all joined together to oust the Bourbons. Yet with the monarch's removal from office the alliance fell apart and the natural polyphony of opinion in society was promptly reinstated. The Republicans wished to establish a democracy with Lafayette as President; the Legitimists still advocated the cause of the traditional monarchy; the Bonapartists now presented the Empire as a beneficent, liberal conception; and in the middle of this confused pattern of claims and counter claims was the bourgeois group which asked for a constitutional monarchy on the English model. Each side of course had its supporters, but the greater economic power of the Constitutionalists plus the clever stage management of their leaders, Talleyrand and Thiers, won the day for them. The Duc d'Orléans under the name of Louis-Philippe, was crowned King of the French People, and for the first time France had a bourgeois government. "The fighting had been done by the workers, but the upper middle classes appropriated the fruits of the victory." [3]

Louis-Philippe was thought by business men to be one of their kind, and to the best of his ability he tried to justify that belief. With a plain grey hat on his head and an umbrella in his hand, the new king seemed to be a royal personification of all the moderate, domestic virtues that the middle class held dear.[4] Of aristocratic blood, yet homely and simple in his ways, he was a man of the new world who subscribed to the constitutional principle of a "throne surrounded by republican institutions." Dedicated to keeping the peace abroad and to providing an atmosphere conducive to a prosperous economic life at home, his reign was a constant search for the golden mean—the *juste milieu* which the liberal bourgeoisie regarded as the only sensible standard to follow.

The bourgeois state, in the opinion of its leaders, should be organized as efficiently and should observe the same strict economy in its operations as any commercial establishment. A thorough revision of the civil administration, therefore, was one of the first orders on the calendar of the incoming ruler. It was necessary to replace the die-hards of the *Ancien Régime* with more liberal-minded officials and to bring the policies of each department into harmony with the general trend of the administration. Furthermore, in keeping with the doctrines of laissez-faire economics propounded earlier by Adam Smith and warmly championed by the business and financial interests of 1830, the questions of where and how to limit the state's activities and expenditures were given much attention.

Among the more costly public institutions were the government-supported theaters, all of which received their due share of criticism at this time. The press, unrestricted again after the abortive attempts to muzzle it during the Restoration, was "generally opposed to the administration [of the theaters] by the state. The subsidized stage was roundly condemned in the name of liberty and in the name of economy." [5] The Opéra, in particular, was a fair target for the liberals because most of its earlier administrative history is one long account of privilege and bad management.

Since June 28, 1669, when Abbé Perrin received his letters patent from Louis XIV, the lyric theater in France had been maintained as a strict monopoly except for a few years during the period of the Revolution (1789). Perrin's authorization states that he may "establish Academies of Music in Paris and in other cities of the kingdom for the purpose of presenting theatrical works in song, as is the practice in Italy, Germany, and England." His privilege was scheduled to extend for twelve years "with the right to collect from the public such sums as he considers proper," and all other persons were forbidden to present "similar operas or productions of music using French texts" without his consent.[6]

The next official document concerning the Opéra concession is much the same in content although it is a bit more explicit on certain points. It was issued on March 13, 1672, in favor of Lully (1632–1687), the superintendent of music for Louis XIV, who had contrived in a short space of time to undermine the position of Perrin at court. "Having been informed," said these new letters patent, "that the labor and care expended by the Sieur Perrin have not been able fully to second our intentions, . . . we have decided, for the sake of better results, to permit . . . our dear and well-beloved Jean Baptiste Lulli . . . to establish an Académie Royale de Musique in our great city of Paris." The privilege was granted for the duration of the composer's life and after that was promised to his heirs. Furthermore, all persons of whatever quality or condition were expressly forbidden to enter this theater without paying, and were likewise prohibited from presenting any piece of music "whether with verses in French or in another language without permission in writing from the aforesaid Sieur Lulli." [7]

Under these generous provisions, Lully is said to have earned 800,000 livres in fifteen years of service.[8] His immediate successors, however, proved so inept that a new set of quite precise rules was issued on January 11, 1713, and supplemented on November 19,

1714, which provide that the director of the Académie Royale de Musique shall be subject to the constant control of an inspector general. The latter's function was to review the choice of artists and the assignment of roles at the Opéra, see that the house rules of discipline were observed, put his visa on all decisions of policy, and render an account to the king of any violation of his wishes by the director.[9]

These regulations were of course promulgated because the Opéra had already acquired the habit of being in debt; but in spite of the added supervision, the financial situation of the lyric theater became no better. Every expedient was then used to alleviate its budgetary distress. An order of November 26, 1716, granted to the Opéra the privilege of selling the right to use music in the popular theaters. Permission to give concerts in the Tuileries during Holy-week and Easter-week was awarded in 1724 to Aimé-Danican Philidor with the stipulation that he must pay six thousand livres each year to the Académie.[10] Letters patent of June, 1769 further prohibited the use of music or dance in any other theater, with or without scenery, and forbade any concerts of vocal or instrumental music, or any balls for which an entrance fee was charged, unless permission was received in writing from the director of the Opéra.[11]

Thus the eighteenth century witnessed a perpetual endeavor in France to aid the lyric theater by giving it a strangle hold on the production of music in Paris. With the coming of the Revolution this monopoly was broken temporarily. The famous law of January 13–19, 1791, granted that "any citizen may erect a public theater for the presentation of pieces of all genres" as long as he notifies the municipal authorities of his plans in advance.[12] Naturally, there was at once a great boom in theatrical activity. New playhouses sprang up everywhere. By 1793 there were eighteen of them offering some kind of lyric drama in the city. As Castil-Blaze points out, these houses of the second and third rank performed the very useful function of absorbing many works not of the quality or size required by the official Opéra.[13] Apparently the yoke of privilege was completely shattered. Even then, however, freedom was destined to be illusory; for while a hall could be opened without hindrance, it could also be closed if its productions did not meet the approval of the Commune.

The great latitude allowed officials in this matter may be judged from the Decree of August 2, 1793, which says that: "Any theater presenting pieces which tend to deprave the spirit of the public or to awaken the shameful superstition of royalty shall be closed, and the directors punished according to the full rigor of the law." [14]

As for the Opéra (or the Théâtre des Arts, as it was renamed on April 7, 1794), all details of its administration were placed squarely under the rigid supervision of the government. Article two of the Decree of 27 Vendémiaire, An III (October 18, 1794), ordered the combined Committees of Public Instruction and Finance to draw up rules concerning the number of artists and officers to be engaged, their contracts, and the administrative and accounting methods to be used at the Théâtre des Arts. In addition, it forced the artists and administrators to guarantee a yearly receipt of 688,000 livres, and stated that any deficit should be made up proportionally from their salaries.[15] Such a system obviously was not a model of liberality except as it relieved the minor theaters of the obligation to support the Opéra.

Their independence, however, was short-lived, for all their past ills followed in the train of Napoleon. The Opéra was like a returned *émigré*. The Théâtre des Arts became the Académie Impériale de Musique, and with this change of name it rid itself quickly of its republican garments and put on again the royal livery. An Imperial Decree of June 8, 1806, directed that "the productions of the Opéra, the Comédie-Française and the Opéra-Comique shall be determined by the Minister of the Interior," and ordered further that "no theater shall present in Paris any piece contained in the repertories of these three major houses without paying them a fee which shall be regulated by contract with the sanction of the Minister." [16] Continuing this restrictive policy, the Emperor next ruled that the number of theaters should be reduced to eight, and on two weeks' notice more than twenty-five houses were forced to close their doors. Only one more stroke was necessary to restore the Opéra to the most favored position which it had enjoyed under the old regime. The circle was completed on August 13, 1811, with the reestablishment of the duty collectable by the Académie from "all theaters of the second rank," and in general from "all amusements of whatever kind they may be." Playhouses were taxed one-twentieth of their revenue, while balls, concerts and other such entertainments were ordered to give one-fifth of their gross receipts to the Opéra. Also, no concert was permitted unless the day had been approved by the Superintendent of Theaters after consulting with the director of the Académie.[17] The official lyric theater was now reinstalled more securely than ever in its former seat of privilege, to which it held fast for the duration of the Empire and throughout the whole of the Restoration.

In those years both the monopoly and its method of administration remained constant. Under Louis XVIII the Opéra reverted to its original name of Académie Royale de Musique, but there was no material change in its policy until the July Monarchy. The governing body of the Opéra was fixed by the Imperial Decree of November 1, 1807. At the head was a new officer, the Superintendent of Theaters, whose duty it was to act as overseer of the four major houses of the capitol: the Opéra, the Théâtre-Français, the Théâtre de l'Impératrice and the Opéra-Comique. Subordinate to him then was the local administration of the Académie which was composed of a director, a treasurer, an inspector and a secretary-general, all office-holders of the state.[18]

On paper this scheme of organization appeared satisfactory, but in practice it left something to be desired—perhaps because an excessive amount of authority was vested in the Superintendent of Theaters. All of the directors since 1816—Choron, Persuis, Viotti, Habeneck, Duplantys and Lubbert—seem to have been kept well under the thumb of this higher functionary. Castil-Blaze called them "men of straw . . . directors put in view . . . directors without power and without will who were there only to be directed." [19] No doubt the power of the Superintendent was weighted in the belief that it was necessary to hold a firm rein on the activities of the individual managers in order to protect the government's investment. Certainly, the experience of the past century, during which there was always a deficit at the Opéra, had not inspired any great confidence in the business and executive capacities of the average director.

As it turned out, however, the Superintendent likewise was seldom a storehouse of wisdom or ability. There is nothing to indicate that his qualifications were required to be any different from those of the ordinary political appointee to a non-technical office. Moreover, though he might or might not know anything about the theater, he was usually not content to confine himself to financial or administrative matters. The world of art was his domain and he was free to roam in it at will. An opera director was chosen presumably for his professional competence, but that fact never prevented the Superintendent from imposing his own ideas on the theater if he so desired.

The problems arising out of this system of administration were shown clearly during the last years of the Restoration. Emile Lubbert, who resigned the direction of the Théâtre-Italien in 1826 to take over that of the Opéra, was a man of fine ability. Well-educated and possessing a wide knowledge of music, he seemed to be an excellent choice for the position at the Académie. But he, too, was forced to labor under the handicap of an incompetent superior. The Vicomte Sosthène de la Rochefoucauld, last Superintendent of Theaters before the July Revolution, was a man who was no less a stranger to art than he was to business. Appointed to office by the Minister of the Maison du Roi, the Duc de Doudeauville, who happened to be his father, he "brought to his government of the Académie Royale de Musique all the incapacity of a nobleman. . . . One could dupe him easily, but he would deceive no one." [20] "Always ready to oppose the projects for reform . . . which the . . . complete dilapidation of the Académie rendered indispensable," [21] he made life distinctly hard for the enterprising Lubbert. La Rochefoucauld may have loved the arts, but he apparently was more concerned with preserving the purity of the ballerinas than with conducting the affairs of the theater profitably and well. Gautier referred to him as the "unfortunate and virginal Viscount who lengthened the skirts of the dancers at the Opéra and with his own patrician hands applied a modest plaster to the middle of all the statues." [22] He sought to bring virtue to the Opéra, but only succeeded in continuing its bankruptcy.

During this moral administration the Académie went even deeper into debt than usual, despite the fact that the Restoration government was quite generous with its allotment of funds. Given an annual subsidy of 750,000 francs to which was added about 300,000 francs taken in tribute from the secondary theaters, the Opéra still did not have enough. In the year 1827, it had to go to the civil list for another 966,000 francs to meet its obligations.[23] One is reminded of certain weak managements of the *Ancien Régime,* although few of them were more ineffectual in their handling of finances than the administration ruled by La Rochefoucauld.

Little wonder, then, that after the Revolution of 1830 the new government should have considered it necessary to reorganize the opera house. Everyone talked of economies to be made, and the proposals to pare or discontinue those state expenses classified as luxuries of course put the subsidized theaters in an extremely embarrassing position—a position which was not eased any by the discovery of a final deficit of over a million francs in the Opéra accounts. The disposition of the Académie was a perplexing problem, but of one thing the government was certain: there was enough trouble on other fronts without stirring up more by an extravagant opera policy. "The first years of the July Monarchy, which imposed no fetters on the liberty of the press, were made very difficult and uneasy by incessant disturbances. It was determined not to allow the affairs of the theater to furnish any fresh pretext or food for the criticism of the opposition." [24]

Actually, the Opéra could be handled in only one of three ways: it might be continued in the old pattern with the hope that more adequate managers could be found; it might be turned over completely to private interests; or it might be operated under some kind of an arrangement that combined state and private enterprise. The first plan obviously had too many unhappy memories attached to it to be acceptable. The second was considered too radical a departure, and so the compromise of the third solution was adopted.

In spite of its displeasure with the recent opera management, the government still felt that the Académie was an asset of the state which should not be abandoned. But it was a question whether it would be possible to soothe, at least partially, the advocates of rigid economy and at the same time maintain the opera house in the style to which the public was accustomed. A mere change in the name of the institution or in its administrative personnel would have been nothing unusual since alterations of that sort had been frequent in the period between the Revolutions of 1789 and 1830. And regardless of whether the theater was directed by sans-culottes or by aristocrats like La Rochefoucauld, each season invariably ended with a sizeable deficit. The modification contemplated by Louis-Philippe and his advisors, therefore, was much more basic in its nature. A revision of policy was outlined which proposed to uphold the traditions and dignity of the Opéra while providing an indemnification for the state against managerial incompetence or failure.

In the preceding regime the personal funds of the director were not engaged to the slightest degree. All risks were supported and all deficits were paid by the government. The onus of a failure might lessen the director's reputation without immediately affecting his pocketbook. To the business man of 1830, however, that did not seem to be an equitable arrangement. It was now asked why the state treasury should have to underwrite the incapacity of a theater manager. Would it not be fairer, more economical, and certainly more in accord with the general program of the new administration, to elevate the management of the Opéra to a position of financial responsibility?

These questions were answered in a set of specifications released by the government on February 28, 1831. After placing the royal theaters within the province of the Minister of the Interior, the first Article stated that: "The administration of the Académie Royale de Musique, known as the Opéra, shall be intrusted to a director-entrepreneur, who shall manage it for six years at his own risk and fortune." [25] By this measure the precedent of a century and a half was broken and the Opéra became a field for private exploitation— to the extent, that is, that the director was no longer to be merely a salaried employee, a "foreman at a thousand francs a month," [26] but one whose personal finances were involved in the success or failure of the institution. He had to take his chances with the public exactly the same as any other business man with something to sell. If he interested it in his product, he might make money. If he did not, he had to be prepared to shoulder the loss. Instead of enjoying a privileged situation guaranteed by the royal coffers against loss, the director now was compelled to run the usual business risks.

It is to be noted, however, that the Opéra became a private undertaking only in so far as the manner of its exploitation was altered. In no sense did it become the property of the director. Nor was he allowed to operate it wholly in accordance with his individual whims. He was free to assemble his own staff, choose within certain limits the works he wished to produce,[27] and take any profit that might accrue. Yet in the discharge of his duties he was also to act as an agent of the state.

The Opéra for him was a real field of speculation, particularly after he was deprived of the levies formerly collected from the secondary theaters; [28] but it was not as great a risk as it might have been. Since the day of its founding the Académie had been the official seat of musical culture in France, and the government still felt that the fate of the arts was so closely bound to the institution that it could not be left to ride entirely unsupported on the fluctuations of private trade. Hence the subsidy was continued, although on a gradually decreasing scale. Eight hundred and ten thousand francs were allotted for the first year. The amount was lowered to 760,000 for the second and third years, and for the last three years it was brought down to 710,000 annually. Furthermore, the prestige of the Académie was safeguarded by the provision that: "The entrepreneur shall be held to maintain the Opéra in the state of magnificence and splendor suitable to this national theater." [29]

From the state's point of view it looked as if the problem of the musical stage was adequately resolved. A compromise was effected here as in the government itself. There was still an Académie Royale de Musique just as there was still a monarchy; but it could be said of both that "the form was preserved while the foundations were modified." [30] Liberty was served by releasing the minor theaters from the subjugation of the Opéra. Economy was promoted by reducing the subsidy of the latter and by shifting its exploitation to an entrepreneur who was made strictly accountable for any losses sustained by the house. The establishment of the principle of contractual right in the monarchy was echoed in the new constitution of the lyric theater. Henceforth, responsibility replaced privilege at the Opéra and artistic policy became aligned with the precepts of trade.

III

VERON, THE DIRECTOR

THE STAGE was set at the Opéra and only one element was lacking: a man who had the financial resources and enough confidence in his own ability to undertake the hazards of its management. Lubbert, the last director under the Restoration, was available and wanted the position again, but his candidacy was severely handicapped by the criticism that attached to almost everyone and everything in the administration of La Rochefoucauld. Fortunately for the government, however, there was another aspirant named Dr. Louis Véron who seemed to be more to its taste. Principally known up to that time as the founder of the *Revue de Paris* in 1829, he was quite innocent of any important musical knowledge or experience. Yet his application had very serious marks in its favor. He was free of any of the taint surrounding the Restoration government and its works, he had strong financial backing, and he had demonstrated in his short career that he understood the ways of business. His previous activities were governed by a clear-headed, opportunistic point of view which was quite in harmony with the prevailing bourgeois standards. Urging his own case before the Minister of the Interior, M. le Comte de Montalivet, Véron said: "I was permitted to explain in a few words how a brilliant and skillful direction of the Opéra might be valuable politically at the beginning of the new reign. It was desirable that the foreigner should be attracted to Paris by the fine performances of musical masterpieces, and that he should find the boxes filled with an elegant and tranquil society. The success and the receipts of the Opéra should be a testimony to the stability of the government." [1]

Such logic was bound to appeal to Louis-Philippe's harassed guardians of law and order, but the Opéra was not yet Véron's. In a final cautious move to protect the state, the Minister decided to require a bond of 250,000 francs from the new director. At this point Lubbert dropped out of the competition; for while he had the aid of the Duc d'Orléans, he discovered that his support was in words, not in francs. Véron, on the other hand, enjoyed the more substantial patronage of Alexandre Aguado, the extremely wealthy banker for the Spanish government. The financier, a close friend of Rossini, had such a fondness for music and the theater that it was not enough for him merely to rent a box at the Opéra. He wanted to participate directly in the life there, and in order to do that he was willing to advance 200,000 francs as security for Véron.

The latter, matching his own prudence against the vigilance of the Minister, took ample time to weigh the stakes. "I hesitated for fifteen days," he wrote, "but after reflection I said to myself: The Revolution of July is the triumph of the bourgeoisie. This victorious middle class will be anxious to reign and to amuse itself. The Opéra will become its Versailles, and it will rush there to take the place of the great lords of the exiled court. The plan to make the Opéra at once brilliant and popular appeared to me to have a fine chance for success." [2] Needless to say, upon the conclusion of his deliberations Véron took Aguado's 200,000 francs, added 50,000 from his own pocket, and signed the papers which gave him the direction of the Académie Royale de Musique for the next six years.

At that moment the French lyric theater began a new life. If the elevation of Louis-Philippe to the throne of France represented the triumph of the middle class in politics the selection of Véron to manage the Opéra was a direct extension of bourgeois influence into the world of the musical stage.

Louis Véron, born in Paris on April 5, 1798, was truly a man of his day, a model of the class pushed to the front by the Revolution of 1830. "He was the perfect bourgeois, the bourgeois in all his magnificence, replacing an elevation of spirit by a genius for business, . . . positive, active, pursuing and attaining . . . his double goal:

the possession of solid realities coupled with a display of outward pomp." [3] One finds in his writings the sententious quality of a play by Scribe. Nearly every page is sprinkled with edifying phrases on the necessity of order and the beauties of economy. He knew his epoch as he knew himself and was pleased with both. Feeling that he particularly embodied the ideals and the achievements of the middle class, he proudly gave to his reminiscences the title *Mémoires d'un Bourgeois de Paris*.

Véron began life as the son of a stationer. Prudence and reason governed his father's household, and in his early years he witnessed the practice of all those "fireside virtues whose sole recompense is the assured future of one's children." [4] As befits the hero of a modern success story, "luxury, pleasures, laughter and soft illusions" had no place in his childhood. He received his schooling at the Lycée Impérial and worked for a time in the paternal trade where he became imbued with "the most prudent and reasonable ideas," and where he seems to have developed a sharp taste for money. But he was quick to see that a business like his father's offered him little room for development. Looking about him, he was impressed with the honors received by a neighboring physician and decided then to become a doctor. His studies were successful and in 1823 he was awarded the degree of Doctor of Medicine. Although his subsequent career makes it appear very likely that medicine for him was more of a speculation than a calling, he did go into practice, was appointed physician to the Royal Museums and even published a monograph entitled *Observations on the Diseases of Children*. Véron felt later that his early medical training stood him in good stead because it taught him to work at a problem systematically; but the most easily measured and probably the most valuable result of his life as a doctor was that it encouraged friendship with a pharmacist named Regnault, inventor of a remedy known as "Regnault's Chest Ointment." The apothecary at his death willed his formula to Véron, who, with the help of a friendly word in the press, soon began to realize a large profit from the inheritance. "A little note inserted in the journals spoke of this preparation as a precious discovery for mankind. The strategy was new. People believed the newspapers yet in those days and thus believed also in the ointment." [5] It may be that this marvelous paste never cured a cold, but at least it brought an annual income of several thousand francs to the lucky doctor.

These earnings plus a modest sum he inherited from his father gave wings to Véron's ambition. The medical profession had begun to pall on him and he made up his mind to enter the field of journalism. At first an obscure contributor to the *Conservateur Littéraire* in which the early verses of Victor Hugo were published, he held next a subordinate position on the staff of the *Quotidienne*. From there he went to the *Messager des Chambres* where he essayed theatrical criticism, and in 1829 he struck out for himself and founded the *Revue de Paris*. The direction of this paper established him both socially and financially, and from that time the Véron legend began to take shape.

His subsequent appointment to the Opéra of course did not diminish his stature either in his own eyes or in the eyes of the public; and as his fame grew the ostentation of his life increased. Risen from modest beginnings to a place of consequence in the world by the time he reached his early thirties, he already displayed the signs and the tastes of a thorough parvenu. He has been the subject of so much raillery on this count that one might be tempted to dismiss him as a mere buffoon. Certainly, neither his physique nor his personality appear very engaging. It is quite impossible, in fact, to find a description of him that is not derogatory in some respect. One writer said that he had "a ruddy, smiling face, greedy and sensual lips, an eager eye and a high, sharp and bold voice." [6] His bearing combined "impertinence and unction, an affectation of levity and a touch of arrogance." A fellow journalist called his face "a mould of Regnault paste in a setting of current jelly." [7] Heine pictured him as a "bulky, caricature-like figure, with a head entirely buried in an immense white cravat . . . rolling about insolently at his ease." [8] And still another contemporary derided this "fat man without a neck, but with a large head, sagging cheeks, a pug nose and a protruding stomach, affecting the manners of the roués of the Regency." [9]

Few men of Véron's generation were more often described, criticized, and ridiculed. But that caused him no displeasure, for "he was one of those who preferred to be spoken of badly rather than not at all." [10] Private life did not exist for him. He seemed happy only when caught in the glare of publicity. When director of the *Revue de Paris* (1829–1831) he occupied a modest little apartment of three rooms "where he never received anyone and in which he seldom stayed. He lived in his carriage, a very elegant brougham drawn by two English horses adorned with scarlet ribbons on their ears." [11] Parading himself at every opportunity, he made advertising copy of anything he did and of all he possessed: "of his carriage, his horses, his dinners at the Café de Paris, his shirt collars, even his personal weaknesses." [12]

Véron's carriage and his cravat were known throughout the city. A story circulated that he once received a letter addressed merely to "M. Véron, in his cravat, Paris." [13] The necktie was so enormous that his enemies were certain it must hide some hideous deformity. He was perhaps even more famous, though, for the sumptuous dinners given at his home after he had moved into larger quarters commensurate with his growing importance. On these occasions he entertained not only persons of influence from the business world, but also men of letters and journalists such as Sainte-Beuve, Nestor Roqueplan, Arsène Houssaye, Malitourne, and the composers Auber, Halévy, and Adam. He usually drew upon the theater for his female guests, preeminent among whom was the great actress Rachel, who is said to have included Véron among her lovers. [14]

His domestic chef was Sophie, one of the most celebrated cooks of the day; and he also carried in his entourage various parasites whom his vanity led him to call his headquarters staff. The best known of these sycophants was Comte Gilbert de Voisins, the divorced husband of Marie Taglioni, she who reigned as the leading danseuse of the Opéra. At his dinners, Véron would address himself to the Count "with a tone that the Regent might have taken when speaking to one of his courtiers; . . . 'Monsieur le Comte, do me the favor of announcing the menu!' " [15] "It is wonderful," remarked a critic, "for the son of a stationer to number a Count among his officers." [16]

With his customary grand air, Véron loved to affect "the manners of a bourgeois rajah." Inviting the members of his corps de ballet to supper, he would present each of them at dessert with a package of bonbons wrapped up in a thousand-franc note.[17] At other times he played the role of Maecenas. Saint-Ange of the *Journal des Débats* wrote him a letter saying: "Lend me two thousand francs; you are so prosperous that I may even repay them." [18] He received more than he asked and Véron counted the debt already discharged by this sally of wit.

He often submitted willingly to such minor impositions, particularly if a journalist was involved. Born in the period when the modern power of the press was just beginning to assert itself,[19] he was one of the first to appreciate its potentialities. He said that he founded the *Revue de Paris* because the moment appeared to him propitious for working in literature, and added loftily that a literary periodical must "aid the muses to take prisoners among the common people and among the ignorant." [20] Despite this fine sentiment, however, which did honor to his character of the bourgeois gentleman, there is no doubt that journalism to him was primarily a great commercial force. He understood better than most men of his day the influence that could be wielded by advertising, and he saw in the press an unexploited and unexcelled medium for display. It was inevitable, then, that he should value the publicist as an ally whose good will must be won and kept.

Many people were courted by Véron, but none more than the journalists. From the beginning of his career he persistently cultivated amiable relations with them. In the Café de Paris he presided in state over their table.[21] At his soirées, whose aim was "to amuse his friends and the persons who composed the brilliant clientèle of his theater," [22] the members of the press were always honored guests. With money and with praise he paved the way for his enterprises. "None knew better than he how to flatter the vanity of some and satisfy the appetite for money of others." [23]

Véron's precautions were well taken, for it seems that certain newspaper critics in the period of Louis-Philippe were not above soliciting a bribe from time to time. "You may hear it [the press] bargaining at the coulisses with an audible 'How much?' clinking in money paid, and laughing at its lack of conscience over a third bottle of champagne. . . . Aladdin's ring never worked greater wonders." [24] Heine says it is hardly credible how humbly the virtuosi "beg in newspaper offices for the least crumb of praise, or how they will twist and turn to get it." [25] Jules Janin, the supreme pontiff of criticism during the first years of the July Monarchy, was accused of levying regular imposts on authors and actors. Each première, it was asserted, brought him six to eight thousand francs from fearful playwrights. Worse yet, to avoid bad reviews the "young and beautiful actresses were obliged to lavish their charms and their kisses on this rogue." [26]

Perhaps the most complete pirate of the stage, however, was Charles Maurice, editor-in-chief of the *Courrier des Théâtres*. "He was the Mandrin of the theatrical press, the Cartouche of the feuilleton. His journal was a den of cutthroats. Woe to the director who refused to pay the ransoms demanded by this brigand. . . . Woe to the artist who did not divide his fee with this freebooter. . . . His specialty was the judgment condensed in one line, in one word. Each day a column of his journal was filled with these laconic sentences of death." [27]

One needs only to read a few of the letters addressed to him by various artists to appreciate the power he exercised. The brightest stars of the theater truckled to his malicious pen. "Protect us as you have done in the past," entreated the famous dancers Fanny and Thérèse Elssler. "You are so kind. Your good will makes artists so happy. You will always find these two sisters your completely devoted friends." [28] Mme. Cinti-Damoreau, soprano of the Opéra, thanked "my dear Charles" a thousand times for the gracious words about her that he put in his paper.[29] "For many years you have furnished my first reading matter of the day," revealed the composer Carafa, "and who knows . . . perhaps also my first thought." [30] Even Boieldieu, the great composer of comic operas, had to bend the knee to Maurice. "From time to time," he confessed, "a small notice on *La Dame Blanche* however short it may be, will make Scribe and me very happy; and we wish to thank you again for what, with your usual generosity, you have already said." [31]

Artists and authors suffered from the sting of the critics, but not Véron. "All the journals," he boasted, "lent me the most enthusiastic support, and vied with each other in celebrating both my great qualities as an administrator and my enlightened passion for letters and arts." [32] Maurice himself led the chorus which sang

Véron's praises. The latter's explanation for these attentions was that he was courteous and polite to everyone. "I never sent a ticket to a man of letters without writing a note in my own hand reproaching him for not coming often enough to the Opéra." [33] Véron of course did a great deal more for his newspaper friends than merely observe the social amenities. In addition to wining and dining them lavishly, he undoubtedly crossed the palm of more than one critic with silver. We do not know how much he paid Maurice or any of the others, but the sum was certainly not small. It was related that he once asked a reviewer, known always to be low in cash, to write a notice for a new ballet which was about to be presented. The critic seized a sheet of paper and was soon at work, but Véron stopped him, took from his purse a five hundred franc note and said: "put this under your paper, you will write badly without it." [34] "He gave much money to his enemies and some even to his friends." [35]

From this it would be easy to assume that Véron simply bought a success at the Opéra. That, however, is only partly true. He understood the power of money, he knew the character of the Parisian press, and he put the two together. The results were happy but they would not have been for long if the journalists had not had something more substantial to write about than an oversized cravat and a fancy, horse-drawn carriage. The gaucherie of many of Véron's habits should not be allowed to hide his real capacity which was admitted by his most caustic detractors. This ability was put to good use at the Académie, and within a remarkably short time the institution threw off its lassitude and began one of the most brilliant periods in its history.

Soon after Véron's installation it became evident that the Opéra was not being directed by a financially irresponsible functionary of the government. Not content merely to open his purse and rule from on high, he intervened actively in all details of the organization. It was his practice to keep in constant touch with the personnel of the theater. "I spent every day in my office," he said, "my door was open and I gave audience to all comers." [36] His time was occupied with a perpetual series of conferences with painters, decorators, machinists, musicians, and anyone else connected with the Opéra. No performance took place unless he assured himself that all was in order.

His own zeal was so great that he could afford to require a similar attitude from his subordinates. By his able and energetic administration he eventually made those around him forget his lack of artistic competence.

Under his leadership the bustle of commerce replaced the placid inertia that had characterized the Opéra for so long. There was much to be done if it was to be transformed into a solvent organization, and Véron realized that no half-hearted measures would suffice. He may have begun life as the son of a shopkeeper, but by the time he arrived at France's first musical stage at the age of thirty-three he had long outgrown the tradesman's viewpoint. He was no desperate plunger, for his grand gestures, as we have seen, were not usually based on pure whim. But he was not lacking in audacity and he had no aversion to change if he thought it profitable.

The first thing he observed was that economies could and should be made in several ways. His subsidy was limited and his directorship immediately followed one that had been both royal and generous. Common sense dictated that "it was necessary to reduce the inevitable expenses, since the receipts might easily decrease rather than go up." [37] On examination, he discovered that great savings could be effected in the purchase of materials for the sets and costumes, and still keep them luxurious. Further, he decided that some salaries had to be cut. The leading artists were not touched because they were indispensable and were protected, moreover, by the terms of their contracts; but the members of the orchestra, the chorus, and the corps de ballet were more vulnerable. These were the ones who felt the pinch. Each person was interviewed by the director himself, and though Véron said that his heart bled in sympathy for the entreaties he received, he realized that he had to learn how to say "no" if he were to be successful in his job.[38] Evidently the men of the orchestra took the blow hardest for they sent a petition to the king asking that the Opéra be returned to its old footing. Their request of course was rejected, and when they saw that their hands were tied they calmed down and returned to their posts.

With this personnel problem settled Véron turned his attention to the auditorium. At this point luck came his way in the form of a supplement to the original set of conditions under which he operated.

An additional sum of 100,000 francs was given him to use in refurbishing the theater. His plans, however, called for more than the application of a little paint. He could not alter the architecture of the building, but he did make it more comfortable and better suited to the needs of the public.

Located in the Rue Le Peletier, this theater had been erected about ten years earlier. The former opera house in which the murdered Duc de Berri received the last sacrament on the night of February 13, 1820, had been demolished after that occurrence by injunction of the Archbishop of Paris. A new hall was then built and on August 16, 1821, was opened to the public. "Elegant in its proportions and with marvelous acoustics," [39] it was approximately fifty-three feet across, seventy-three feet long and sixty feet high, and had a stage which was forty feet in width.[40] Its original seating capacity of 1,954 was only about half that of the Metropolitan Opera House in New York, but judging from pictures,[41] its general appearance was quite similar to the American theater.

Continuing the comparison, it is interesting to note that in 1831 in Paris, just as in 1940 in New York, the opera management felt impelled to alter the seating arrangements of the hall to accord with a change in the composition of its clientèle. In each case a move was made to open to a larger public those parts of the theater formerly occupied by a privileged caste. Véron said that he reduced the number of boxes containing six seats and multiplied those having four, since the smaller price of the latter "might better suit the fortunes and the habits of economy of the new 'grands seigneurs' of the third estate who had replaced those of Charles X." [42]

The change in 1831 of course was a reflection of the social upheaval following the Revolution. Parisian society at that time, according to Mme. Emile de Girardin, was divided into at least two distinct worlds. At one pole was a sullen aristocracy and at the other was the reigning bourgeoisie. The first of these worlds was grave and serious, "a depository of ancient virtues and beliefs." Dignity for it had been reduced to a system "which revered the Church, the family and the royalty." The second world was a "chaos of ideas . . . a mélange of incredulity and of prejudices, of little freedoms and of great inhibitions, of obsolete habits and new wants. The first lived for esteem and respect and was bored, while the second lived for pleasure and was amused." [43]

In the latter group were the nouveau riche: men of business, men in the professions, politicians seeking distraction from their daily worries and anxious to prove that money could take the place of birth. During the Restoration they cut no great figure at the Court or at the Opéra. They were dismissed from the one and made uncomfortable at the other. The Opéra was "fashionable but not popular. The bourgeoisie feared to enter its doors. They were ill at ease because the Théâtre de la Rue le Peletier . . . was still an auxiliary of the palace." [44] After the fighting of 1830, however, the situation was very different. Once Louis-Philippe was enthroned the middle classes began to make up for the slights they had suffered. They wished to take their place at the banquet table, "to install themselves in the new monarchy as in their own fief." [45] Moreover, they wanted to be domiciled in the Académie, the traditional home of the aristocracy.

The Revolution gave them entrance to the palace and it also gave them possession of the lyric theater. "From 1831 the rich bourgeoisie took up their residence at the Opéra." [46] Véron was their representative, and he was fully aware of the meaning of his appointment. He believed, as did his sovereign that "the middle classes are not all of society, but they are its force." [47] They understood Véron and he, being of the same circle and with much the same kind of taste, knew how to please them.

He also realized that he had to attract them if he were to avoid going into debt. The subsidy, he felt, was insufficient to guarantee him against loss unless his receipts from the Opéra greatly exceeded any of the sums taken in during the best years of the Restoration. It obviously behooved him to use every possible means at his disposal to enhance the drawing power of the theater. Being well acquainted, however, with the tricks of publicity, the task presented to him no unusual difficulties.

Just as Véron turned his own private life into a public spectacle, so he called attention to the Opéra by removing the "no admittance" sign from the stage door and by transforming the traditional Opéra balls into brilliant carnivals whose luxury and licence became the talk of Paris. La Rochefoucauld by a special edict in 1825 had forbidden the glamorous area backstage to any but employees, but that was soon changed. Realizing the fascination exercised on most habitués of the theater by all the little mysteries of the wings and the foyers, Véron opened to his subscribers "the door to the gardens of Armide." He believed, and rightly, that this move could not fail to increase the receipts of the box office. "It was especially on the days of ballet that the ticket-holders, who had the privilege of entering the seraglio and who knew well its windings, thronged to render homage to beauty and the dance." [48]

The colorful balls given at the Académie were an even greater advertisement for the house. "This was the heyday of the masked ball. On the approach of the carnival season, theaters and restaurants were converted into ballrooms." [49] But with all this competition, the gatherings sponsored by the Opéra were easily the most spectacular and renowned. Established at that theater on December 31, 1715, by the Regent, who "more than any one else, was fond of these entertainments," [50] they continued to be held until prohibited by a Committee of Public Welfare on February 11, 1790. However, in 1799 they were permitted again, although disguises were not allowed; and in the following year the mask returned. At the time of Véron "the old Opéra ball, boring, formal, pretentious . . . had ceased to exist." [51] In its place was a kind of entertainment which was part dance and part rout. Nothing was neglected to make it brilliant and animated. The famous Musard, orchestra leader of the Variétés who had won celebrity for the verve with which he conducted the can-can, was engaged by the Opéra to organize and direct its balls.[52] There were "lotteries, large orchestras, . . . Spanish dancers, pageantry, . . . and an unheard-of luxury of lighting." [53] Crowds stormed the hall. One met men from the bench, from letters, the arts, the bar, and from business; [54] but others, too, of a different sort were also in attendance. The entrance barriers had been lowered and the Opéra was invaded by a host of dubious characters, "by dancers from the public houses and by girls who were under the surveillance of the police." [55] Vagrants of the public balls and seekers after adventure jostled one another in their masks. The Opéra ball was now a "mélange of comic interludes, strange actions, of elegant costumes contrasted with ragged apparel, of excited familiarities and of frenzied cries. In the foyer and in the corridors the conversations showed the effects of the unconstraint of the dance. No one troubled to lower his voice for either trivial pleasantries or for licentious allusions . . . intrigues were plotted and undone aloud, without modesty or pretense." [56] "The Opéra ball was a field of opportunity for a venal gallantry. . . . It was not merely a mad orgy as some thought; but a vast and opulent setting for a trade in debauchery and prostitution." [57] These were nights dreamed of by the working girl. They lacked all taste, but they accomplished their purpose. The Opéra became the most talked-of theater in Paris.

It also became the best attended. In 1829 one lamented that "the glorious days of the Opéra are long since past." [58] It "was dying of languor, sleeping on its subsidy." [59] Two years later, however, it was the most glamorous theater in the city and on the Continent. "There is nothing now in Europe like the Académie Royale de Musique," [60] said the Englishman, Chorley. "In Paris," reported *La Revue des Deux Mondes,* "one's mind is either on politics or the Opéra . . . the Assembly echoes with threats and complaints; a thousand sinister prophecies disturb the air: all that is fine for the day. Night comes and one thinks no more of such things. Behold the crowd rushes to the Opéra." [61] Boxes were sharply disputed. "The taste for music, or to be more exact, for opera, has seized everyone: each wants his box at the Opéra, some once, others twice, and still others three times a week. The solicitors, attorneys, and stockbrokers, who wish to show their rank, appear on two nights: on Monday, the petit jour, with their wives, and on Friday, the grand jour, with their mistresses. . . . For the Bourse nothing is too fine, nothing too expensive: it disputes the best boxes . . . with ambassadors, dukes, marquis, and with the dandies." [62]

Some members of the aristocracy recoiled before this bourgeois wave and transferred their affections to the Théâtre-Italien, but it was not a total exodus. Many still retained their old seats at the Opéra. They could be seen especially in the famous *loge infernale,* for in it were assembled most of the elegant men-about-town. Dandies like the Comte Fernand de Montguyon came attended by their young satellites. Balzac was often there along with the Marquis du Hallay, Conrad de Lagrange, Lautour-Mézeray, Charles de Boigne, James Fazy, the young Arsène Houssaye, Nestor Roqueplan, and many others. Here "one sought to distinguish himself at any cost." Lautour-Mézeray always wore a white camelia in his buttonhole. Another habitué invented a new manner of applauding. "Holding his gloved hands far apart and then bringing them together quietly, his applause could be seen from a distance without the risk of being confused with the noise of the crowd. . . . What tales are told about this box! It is even said that the gentlemen in it had constructed opera glasses that enlarged objects thirty-two times and from which the tights of the dancers kept no secrets." [63]

Between acts, the fashionable world of the boxes overflowed into the foyer. It was then in its full glory. "All of society wishes to see itself in the mirrors of the lobby. . . . Elegant youths in yellow gloves push towards the front." One saw statesmen and men from industry. "The bourgeoisie, familiar now with all the names and with all the reputations, mingles without constraint or embarrassment in this brilliant concourse of contrasts. . . . The diplomatic corps is as punctilious in its etiquette there as in the meeting of a Congress. . . . The chronicle of this lobby sums up all the politics of Europe. . . . Every distinguished stranger soon finds his way there. . . . For high political circles the foyer of the Opéra is an indispensable resting place between the dining room and the salon." [64]

Véron could rightly say that under his direction the Opéra became the show place not only of France but of Europe, and the favorite meeting ground for society. This was true in 1831, a few months after he assumed the leadership of the theater. And it was still true in 1835 when he resigned. One journal said that the Opéra "is almost our sole glory." [65] Another called it "the most brilliant and the most fortunate of theaters. . . . In this century of disillusionment and ruin, music has conserved its prestige." [66]

Only twice between 1672 and 1835 was a director of the Opéra lucky and clever enough to gain such unconditional ratification of his program by the public, and only twice did he complete his term of office with a profit. Lully accomplished the feat at the beginning of that one hundred and sixty year period and Véron duplicated it at the end. Each found the secret of administration which enabled him to amuse his audience and at the same time keep his expenses within bounds. Lully, of course, was prompted by a desire to further his own career in composition as well as to make money. Véron was simply a business man—for all his protestations to the contrary—with no real artistic gifts or aspirations. He sought the Opéra position because he thought the time was ripe for a profitable exploitation, and he relinquished it before the expiration of his contract because he was convinced that his earnings in the theater had reached their peak. "I did not remain there too long," he said; ". . . I prudently left the establishment when the subsidy was diminished." [67] In this speculation as in others where failure is more the rule than the exception, Véron enriched himself. And he did so because he joined to a talent for making his fortune the equally important ability to conserve it.

His attitude was at once practical for himself and representative of the bourgeois spirit which engulfed the Opéra. Véron was a man of his time. "His personality," remarked an observer, "will remain one of the most characteristic of our period." [68] In his person "he offers an assemblage of general traits which constitute the bourgeoisie of 1830–1848." [69] His weaknesses magnified their failings just as his achievements crowned their successes. As a faithful agent of his class he made business an art and art a business. He was a living proof of Figaro's dictum that "To know how is worth more than to know." But in the last analysis, Véron, with all his absurdities, was a useful man, for he rescued the Opéra from the slough of routine into which it had fallen. If he was not inspired by the most elevated ideals, he at least provided the material conditions necessary for the establishment of grand opera. And in so doing, he gave to the French lyric theater a splendor and a prosperity which it had never known before.

IV

THE PERSONNEL OF
THE OPERA

T HE LAST Opéra administration during the Restoration left the government nothing but a towering debt, yet it bequeathed to Véron one valuable legacy without which he could not have worked: a company of artists in many ways second to none.

Véron was particularly fortunate to have the key positions in his cabinet filled by able and experienced men. His chorus master was no less a person than Jacques Fromentin Halévy (1799–1862) whose own composition, *La Juive,* played an important part in the early history of grand opera and gave a triumphant flourish to the close of Véron's reign. A professor of harmony at the Conservatoire, his career also included a term as *maestro al cembalo* at the Théâtre-Italien before he came to the Académie in 1830.

As leading conductor Véron had François Antoine Habeneck (1781–1849), a brilliant violinist, former director of the Opéra from 1821 to 1823, conductor at the same house since 1824, founder of the famous Concerts du Conservatoire and probably best known to musical history as the man who introduced the symphonies and quartets of Beethoven to the Parisian public. Under his direction the orchestra at the Opéra became a model in its day. "What brilliancy is there in its violins. . . . Nor are the wind instruments inferior . . . if their tone be not of the highest quality, and partakes somewhat of that thin shrillness which seems generic to all wind tones (the human voice included) in France, they are still admirable for their certainty and for their freedom from grossness. . . . Then there is a uniform but well-proportioned care in finish and consent of execution—a sensitiveness as to every nicest gradation of time. . . . It is a machine, in short, in perfect order, and under the guidance of experience and intellect; for these, as regards French music, are personified in M. Habeneck. Nothing can exceed his perfect sway over his forces." [1] Berlioz once had his difficulties with Habeneck; [2] but Rossini is said to have admired his quick eye and his "communicative warmth," and Meyerbeer ostensibly never rested easier after his dinner than when he knew without doubt that Habeneck would conduct. [3]

Happily, there were artists now on the stage as well as in the pit who were worthy of the Académie Royale de Musique. The troupe included brilliant performers in both dance and song. The dancers, always important figures in French opera, had as their leader the fabulous Marie Taglioni. Making her debut at the Opéra in 1827, she danced "from triumph to triumph. Perhaps there has never existed another example of a danseuse so applauded, so honored, so adored." [4] Although somewhat ill-shaped and lacking any of the exterior advantages which invite success, she conquered all by the perfect beauty of her art. *La Sylphide* (1832), the ballet by Nourrit and Schneitzhoffer which produced her greatest role, "merged her qualities with her defects; she was thin, it made her a spirit, it condensed her into vapor. . . . La Sylphide became the personification of Mademoiselle Taglioni." [5] She was "more than a dancer, the most perfect that had ever appeared on the stage of the Opéra; she was the dance itself. Correct without coldness, aerial without effort, . . . her dancing spoke to the spirit, while the old dance did not speak even to the senses, addressing itself only to the eyes. Before Taglioni, dancing was only a métier, that of leaping as high as possible, of pirouetting as a top. She appeared and the trade became an art, the old school crumbled." [6] Taglioni was supported by Perrot, the premier danseur, and rivalled after 1834 by Fanny Elssler, but during most of Véron's administration she was supreme.

Her dancing was a handsome complement to song at the Opéra, for the latter art also was rejuvenated in the closing years of the Restoration. The long drought of good singing which had afflicted the Académie since the early days of Spontini's career was over. That stage was no longer the wasteland of vocal art that it had been for more than a decade. It could hold its head up again in the assurance that its personnel were equal to the demands placed upon them. But if the art of singing at the Opéra was revived, it was also changed in the process from what it had ever been before. The well of native tradition, whose source was the grand declamatory mode of Lully, had run dry; and the overflowing stream of Italian song was diverted to the replenishment of the Académie.

A movement begun many years before had reached its climax. From the period almost two centuries earlier when Cardinal Mazarin first called to Paris a company of Italian singers a constant pressure from across the Alps was exerted on French musical taste and vocal technique. The initial wedge was driven by the performance under the Cardinal's auspices of Sacrati's opera *La Festa teatrale della finta Pazza* on December 14, 1645. This did not prove decisive, however, in determining the course of French opera because the powerful personality of Lully intervened. Steeping himself in the ideals of declamation which were practiced at the Comédie-Française in the performances of Racine, he adapted their methods to the musical stage. And as the classical playwrights formed their own school of acting, so he, in producing the *tragédie lyrique*, trained his interpreters and founded a style of singing which was the expression of his theatrical principles.

After his death and throughout most of the eighteenth century Lully's conception remained strong. The Italian wing, though, was never silent. Periodically it would surge forward and become involved in one of the "wars" that dot French operatic history. The most famous of these was occasioned by the arrival in Paris in 1752 of an Italian group to present Pergolesi's *La Serva Padrona*. Another was the Gluck-Piccini quarrel which took place later in the century. During the Revolution, when people's minds were on something besides vocal roulades, the Italian performers emigrated, but in 1801 they returned and received a warmer welcome than ever. Napoleon, who had little or no taste for French music or its interpreters, staffed his chapel of the Tuileries entirely with Italian singers and gave official status to the Théâtre-Italien which henceforth was the home of ultramontane opera in France.

As the Italians became more firmly entrenched and waxed in success the French school fell into a decline. At the Académie "the *tragédie lyrique*, disfigured by the successors of Gluck, Sacchini, and Spontini, had arrived in the last days of the Empire . . . at the final degree of nullity." [7] The singing, likewise, had deteriorated into what the Italians called the *urlo francese* or the French howling. "I heard the last generation of these interpreters of the *tragédie lyrique*," said the critic Paul Scudo, "and can vouch that the greatest exaggerations are nothing in comparison with the barking of Dérivis and Nourrit père." [8] "The artists, as old and worn out as the theater itself, sang (or rather shrieked) without voices, without teeth, deeply wrinkled and shabbily costumed. The most celebrated members of the company, Mme. Branchu, Lays, the elder Nourrit, and one or two others, were tolerated out of sympathy and charity, for it was known that these former favorites were to be pensioned within a few years. When I first saw them [in 1817]," remarked Sophie Leo, "they were truly pitiable." [9]

Apparently France could not help itself, for in a desperate effort to inject new life into the Académie, Rossini, the chief of the Italians, was called upon in 1826. Engaged to write for the French theater, his first task was to try to teach the cast how to sing his style of music. "The nature of their talent was analogous to the works which they presented," [10] and the older artists, "accustomed to the tragico-lyric declamation, were not young enough to mend their ways. The least vocalization baffled them." [11] The difficulties encountered by Rossini may be imagined when it is recalled that the title role of *Guillaume Tell* had to be written originally for a singer by the name of Dabadie. Spoken of by Fétis, the founder and editor of the *Revue Musicale*, as one who tranquilly pursued his trade without rivalry and without warmth,[12] his portrait was filled out by Charles de Boigne who described him as an estimable *père de famille* with a patriarchal figure, the bearing of a bourgeois and a light voice—"a fat, coarse singer on whom the vogue lit an instant during the last days of the Restoration." [13]

At the Académie there were other performers equally weak and inflexible, but Rossini discovered two male singers capable of taking leading roles who were not only gifted but receptive. Each had had previous training in the Italian style, but neither had fully realized his possibilities. Nicolas Prosper Levasseur, a bass, made his debut at the Opéra as far back as 1813, and found quite soon that the old repertory was unfavorable to the method of singing he followed. Thereafter he appeared in London, in Italy where he had a part in Meyerbeer's early work, *Margherita d'Angiù*, at the Théâtre-Italien in Paris, and finally again at the Opéra. His talent, however, did not unfold entirely until he began to sing in such pieces as Rossini's *Le Comte Ory* (1828) and *Guillaume Tell* (1829), and later in Meyerbeer's *Robert le Diable* (1831). His success then was complete. "No one had more zeal, more intelligence, and what respect for the text, what incorruptible fidelity in his interpretations." [14]

Adolphe Nourrit, a tenor, proved even more outstanding. His accomplishments, in fact, were so unusual and so varied that he became in his way as much of a legend in Paris as Véron himself. A pupil of the famous singing teacher, Manuel Garcia, Nourrit made his debut at the Opéra in 1821 when only twenty years of age. As Pylade in Gluck's *Iphigénie en Tauride* he did so well that "criticism was disarmed." [15] Yet a few years later the works of Rossini presented him with an entirely new problem whose solution required that he add to his equipment "a more complete science of singing." [16] Realizing the deficiencies in his training, Nourrit had the courage to place himself once again under the tutelage of his former teacher. Moreover, he turned eagerly for advice to Rossini, whose wide experience in all kinds of theaters—good and bad—made his counsel invaluable. The effect of this further study was such that after the first performance of Rossini's *Le Siège de Corinthe* (1826) the composer was completely reassured about the singing.[17]

While Nourrit was concentrating on the improvement of his vocal technique, however, he was active also in many other ways. He looked upon his profession "as a priesthood and made of his art a sort of religion." [18] Everything concerned with music or the theater was food for his mind. He was an assiduous student of acting and stagecraft. "Costume, attitude, by-play, nothing was neglected by

Nourrit." [19] For him the study of his own role in an opera was only the beginning, the least he could do. After that he worked on all the other parts, occupied himself with the thousand details of the *mise en scène,* and was a constant and welcome adviser to the management as well as to the librettist and composer. "Nourrit was a good counselor at the general rehearsals, and his own roles gained much from the shrewd changes that he proposed." [20] Ending the fourth act of *La Juive* (1835) with an air instead of with a chorus was the result of a recommendation he made to Halévy. And it was he also who conceived the idea of concluding the fourth act of *Les Huguenots* with a grand duet.

His mind was never at rest. Not content to work only in opera, he found time to introduce the songs of Schubert to the salons of Paris and to write the scenario for *La Sylphide* (1832), one of the most popular ballets in the repertory of the time. Outside the theater "he was keenly interested in all the new ideas; De Maistre, George Sand, Lamennais contended for his mind." [21] His interest in politics even took an active turn during the July Revolution. He marched, sword in hand, at the head of a company of militia and sang the *Marseillaise* from the top of the barricades. Thereafter, to satisfy the popular clamor, he went from theater to theater singing patriotic songs which the people repeated after him in chorus with wild enthusiasm.[22] Little wonder, then, that by the time of Véron's accession the public had so taken Nourrit to its heart that "he moved surrounded by a brilliant crescendo of success and renown." [23]

For some time he ruled almost alone on the Opéra stage. Until the debut of Marie-Cornélie Falcon in 1832 there was no female singer who could rightly be called his equal partner. The Académie employed some capable women, but no great artists. In the troupe were Mme. Dabadie, Mlle. Constance Jawureck, Mme. Dorus-Gras and especially Mme. Cinti-Damoreau. The latter, called to the Opéra from the Théâtre-Italien at the instigation of Rossini, was described, in fact, as "the perfect model of the art of song"; [24] but neither she nor any of her companions was a complete artist like Nourrit and none was able to capture the fancy of the theater public. Mme. Damoreau, "despite her admirable talent, never exercised any influence on the receipts of the Opéra; let her sing, or let Mlle.

Jawureck, there was not one centime more, not one centime less." [25]

It was to Véron's credit as well as to the benefit of his purse that he engaged the phenomenal Falcon in the same year that she finished her studies at the Conservatoire. Her debut in Meyerbeer's *Robert le Diable* was a tremendous success. She won immediate acclaim both for her beauty and for her artistry. "Cornélie Falcon had an olympian profile, regular, a little cold, but admirable. Her black eyes, black hair, firm lips, her tall figure and her elegant bearing reminded one of a Roman empress." [26] Her voice was "of wide compass, limpid, wonderfully sweet and genuine, and yet capable of the most grandiose effects." [27] As befitted a student of Nourrit, "her singing was a model of diction and of expression. . . . Before Cornélie Falcon there had not been seen on the stage of the Académie Royale an artist uniting in the one person so many natural means, so much talent of execution, so much distinction and beauty. . . . Falcon in Robert was an astonishment and a triumph." [28] "Modern art saluted in her its inspired priestess." [29]

In Cornélie Falcon the Opéra had an artist who could balance the fame of Maria Malibran and Henriette Sontag at the Théâtre-Italien. It need be said no longer that the Opéra "is supported on the legs of its dancers." [30] The vocal style at the Académie which had been forty years behind its time was brought up to date. "Levasseur, Adolphe Nourrit, and Mme. Damoreau succeeded Dérivis, Nourrit père, and Mme. Branchu, and the art of singing . . . drove out that bombastic and degenerate declamation which belonged neither to tragedy nor to music." [31] Fétis could not say now as he did in 1827 that the Opéra troupe was "a sad subject of reflection," [32] for the Académie, "wholly regenerated, possessed a complete company of excellent singers whose dramatic talent had been put to the proof." [33]

By 1831 the revolution in French singing was an accomplished fact. Full assimilation of Rossini's style led to such improvement in the vocal technique at the Opéra that it was said the French singers interpreted the music of the Italian master as if they came from La Scala. [34] But the revolution amounted to more than merely acquiring facility in foreign methods. As Rossini in *Guillaume Tell* fitted his own style of composition to the dramatic and scenic conceptions of the French lyric theater, so the leading singers at the Opéra joined their new learning to their old inheritance. Nourrit, in particular, illustrated the merger of the two elements which resulted in a style that was new but quite *en rapport* with the sympathies and tastes of the public. From the standpoint of pure vocal technique he had his superiors, but "no one was ever better suited to the French Opéra." [35] He was "a true French singer, the singer of a people to whom the musical emotions alone do not suffice, who ask for an interesting poem and for attractive decorations and costumes." [36] Nourrit was "the first to understand that something besides declamation was possible at the Opéra, and to take a just middle ground between the exaggerated dramatic expression of the old French school and the excessive embellishments of the Italian singers." [37] Upon this foundation of French declamation wedded to Italian *bel canto* the vocal line of grand opera was built, and in Nourrit and Falcon it found its ideal interpreters.

AUGUSTE AND THE CLAQUE

The artists of the Opéra enjoyed a success which was both great and fully deserved. Yet it is no reflection on them to say that their work might very possibly have received less acclaim were it not for the labors of the Opéra's publicity department, centering in the program of the claque. Methodically organized and directed, the latter furnished a constant support both to the performers and to the productions in which they appeared.

In the Paris of 1831 the claque was as formidable as the Opéra was brilliant. It was the spark that ignited the vast charge of public approval which greeted the Meyerbeerian grand opera. More than that, the action of the claque was itself like a bit of grand opera— played off stage, but guided by the same principles of effect as the spectacle on the other side of the footlights.

If, like modern advertising, it was the butt of occasional jibes, the claque was nevertheless recognized as an absolute business necessity by all theatrical producers in Paris. In particular, it enjoyed the esteem and the continuous patronage of the director of the

Académie Royale de Musique. The claque took its place alongside the press as one of Véron's most powerful and most devoted aids. He considered it unthinkable to present a work without first making the necessary arrangements for stimulating applause. Such preliminary dispositions were as much a part of the production scheme as anything that took place on the stage, and they received just as careful thought.

Véron himself ordinarily reviewed everything that went into the preparation of a work, down to the last detail; but in all matters relating to the claque he relied completely upon the judgment of its leader, Auguste Levasseur. The latter, whose fame in the theater was so great that he became known simply as "Auguste," gave counsel to Véron and was the intimate of most of the important singers, dancers, and composers of the time. "He lived—indeed, he could only live at the Opéra. . . . Large, robust, a veritable Hercules in size, and gifted with an extraordinary pair of hands, he was created and put into the world to be a claqueur." [38] Lest this seem to be a minor distinction, it should be mentioned that his income from that profession was estimated by his contemporaries at between twenty and thirty thousand francs a year—a figure which compared favorably with that paid the most prominent members of the company.

The sum included fees from a great many sources. A debut, for instance, was usually the occasion for a contract between the artist's family or patron and Auguste, in which the charge was governed by the pretensions of the debutant. The première of an opera also yielded rich tributes to Auguste from the artists appearing in the new work, and the authors themselves frequently "deposited offerings on this altar to glory." [39] In addition, a regular impost of tickets was levied on the administration of the Opéra.

Some of Auguste's payment was in cash and some in tickets. The authors and artists contributed in both ways, while the administration paid only in tickets. Mlle. Lise Noblet, the dancer who created the role of Fenella in Auber's opera, *La Muette de Portici* (1828), is said to have given him something like fifty francs a performance over a period of fifteen years.[40] Other artists may not have paid so much, but nearly all had contracts with him, and, according to

Charles de Boigne, all handed over to him their *billets de service* (two to six tickets per performance given to each artist).[41] The director, on his part, gave Auguste at least one hundred parterre tickets for a première, forty to fifty if a work previously given still required assistance, and only ten to twenty when the piece in question already had a sure audience. The lion's share of the booty was kept by Auguste; the rest he doled out to his subordinates. The tickets were then either sold or given away, the recipient in either case being obligated to join the claque and applaud at command.

The plotting of those commands was like an exercise in military strategy. Theater-goers today are probably familiar with the practice known as "papering the house" employed by many artists in the concert field, and the claque is no stranger to the Metropolitan Opera House; but in this country there is nothing comparable to the carefully worked out system for stimulating applause that is associated with the name of Auguste. Applause to some may be only a spontaneous gesture of approval; or in the tradition of the American concert hall, it may be merely a stereotyped social gesture which is part of an uncritical attitude towards art. To Auguste, however, it was a nice calculation and distribution of effective causes in the form of persons engaged to respond appropriately at a given signal. Naturally, the amount of stimulation to be applied depended on the event and the extent of the reward.

The initial presentation of a new work was of course the occasion when Auguste's help assumed the greatest importance. In order to formulate an intelligent plan of action he would make a careful study of the book, the music, and the *mise en scène,* and would attend rehearsals regularly. During the day he perfected the arrangements with his assistants, consulted with the management, spoke with the artists—most of whom favored him with the greatest deference—and at night he took his customary post in the parterre. Numerous campaigns had made him an able tactician, but he always prepared long in advance, never leaving anything to chance. His final preliminary move was to hold a long conference on the eve of the first performance with the director in the latter's office. At that time, Véron said, "We would pass in review the whole work, from the first scene to the last. I never imposed my opinions, I listened to his. He estimated, he judged everything—dance and song—according to his personal impressions." [42] Auguste then would trace out the program he had mapped for the gradation of the applause, and if Véron was satisfied the preparations were considered complete.

On the day of the performance, Auguste, like a wise general, made sure that his army entered the field before the audience did, since he "wanted complete freedom to put into execution his strategic plans, to dispose his advance guard, to assure the position of his reserves, and to defend the flanks and the rear of his army by hardened troops." [43] The public thus found itself honeycombed and surrounded by claqueurs, and over all reigned Auguste, dressed for the event in conspicuous clothes of colors chosen to attract the eyes of everyone.

There is no point in overestimating the intelligence of the claque as a whole, but it is clear that the duties of its leader required something more of him than a large pair of hands. It is true that he was a mercenary soldier at the service of the highest bidder, yet he was also an honest broker and one who kept the standards of his performance high. "I have seldom seen a more majestic demeanor than his," said Berlioz. "Never was there a more intelligent or a braver dispenser of glory enthroned in the pit of a theater. . . . One has often admired, but not enough in my opinion, the marvelous talent with which Auguste directs the great works of the modern repertory and the excellent advice that he gives on many occasions to the authors." [44] "Although he never refused the number of handclaps desired, he had his own particular admirations and was not, like many men in higher places, the dupe of the noise that he made." [45] The claqueurs of the Opéra, indeed, were "the most civilized in the world, and Auguste, the venerable chieftain of the claque during the administrations of Véron and Duponchel, will be remembered as the soul of moderation and as a splendid model to imitate." [46]

The sum of his formal knowledge concerning the arts was probably quite small. He was neither a lettered man nor a musician, yet he does not seem to have been a total stranger to either literature or music. Frequent attendance at the theater had developed a flair for opera which allowed him to make quite accurate judgments about the effectiveness and the possible reception of new productions. Before the first performance of *Les Huguenots* (1836) he wrote to the director: "I am quite content with the new opera. It is a pleasure to work for such a piece." [47] He knew the strength and the weakness of works he seconded; he knew his public; and he put this knowledge at the disposal of his employers. There is every reason to believe that they valued his assistance.

Although it might be difficult today to find many apologists for the claque, in Auguste's time it was not only accepted openly in all Parisian theaters, but by some people its role was even considered worthy of respect.

Théophile Gautier (1811–1872), one of the 19th century's most acute critics, upheld the claqueur as a man who "renders as much service to the public as to the administration. If he has sometimes protected mediocrity, he has often sustained a new, adventurous work, swayed a hesitant public, and silenced envy. Moreover, in delaying the failure of pieces that have necessitated much expense, he has prevented the ruin of a vast enterprise and the despair of a hundred families. He enlivens performances that without him would be dull and cold; he is the lash of the whip that makes the actor rebound and precipitates him towards success; he gives heart to the young, trembling debutant. . . . In short, the claqueur represents the thoughtfulness of the director for the public which one supposes to be too genteel and well-gloved to applaud by itself." [48]

In the opinion of Véron, too, the mission of his paid applauders was in no way exorbitant or dangerous. On the contrary, it was decidedly beneficent. "You have," he told them, "a fine part to play. You must put an end to all quarrels, come to the succor of the weaker and defend them against the stronger, give an example of politeness and good conduct, and stop by all means the unjust coalitions against the artists on the stage or against the works presented." [49] The claque thus was to be both a model of decorum and an institutional watchdog.

Véron's statement is enlightening provided we discount on his part any philanthropic zeal or intention. He used the claque because he thought it profitable. He undoubtedly wanted his audiences to be well-mannered, but not merely for their own good. His interest in the public's deportment was motivated by a realization that cabals in the theater can very easily wreck the best-laid plans of a director. Theatrical feuds and public disturbances over the relative merits of artists or compositions perhaps indicate a lively concern with art, but they are not always an aid to the box office. Véron, whose expressed object was to make the Opéra the delight of the bourgeoisie, saw clearly that to do this he could not afford the dubious luxury of allowing his theater to become a battleground. For that reason, full use was made of the claque and every precaution was taken to reduce to a minimum the hazard of a militantly divided audience.

To the makers of grand opera the public was a prospective customer to be flattered and wooed rather than warred upon; while to the Romanticists of the drama it was an enemy to be shelled, then taken by storm. "One has to battle for his thoughts, battle for love, battle to compose an epic poem. . . . The ink itself must smell of powder; philosophical truth is proclaimed in explosions of oratory and is sustained [to the sound of] chairs that are being smashed." [50] The first performance of a drama by Victor Hugo appears to have been less an event of pleasure than an affair of honor between deadly antagonists. Read, for instance, Gautier's account of the opening night of *Hernani* (February 25, 1830). The services of the professional claque were obstinately refused by Hugo on the ground that the members were Classicists at heart with a taste for writers like Casimir Delavigne (1793–1843) and Scribe. And in their place, small squads of disciples were posted in the theater, each man carrying as a pass a square of red paper with the word "Hierro" inscribed upon it. Concerning the rest of the house, Gautier said that one needed only to cast a glance at the public to see that this was no ordinary performance; that two systems, two parties, two armies, two civilizations, were facing each other filled with mutual hatred of the intense literary kind, ready to come to blows and longing for a fight.[51]

Open hostilities of that kind were welcomed by the young warriors of Romanticism, but were not at all to the taste of the director of the Opéra. In Véron's theater whatever smacked of partisan bitterness was shunned like the plague. It was not only pleasanter but much better business to run a middle-of-the-road course designed to please as many and offend as few people as possible. He himself sedulously avoided expressing publicly such opinions as might reflect on any composer, and to the best of his ability he attempted to keep the opera house free of acrimonious debate. Hence he felt it eminently desirable to ease the way of his productions by dealing bountifully with the claque. Acting on the ancient principle that nothing succeeds like success, Véron went to great lengths to surround his administration with an air of affluence and invincibility. In his four and a half years at the Académie he brought out only two operas that deserved to be called "triumphs": Meyerbeer's *Robert le Diable* in 1831 and Halévy's *La Juive* in 1835. Yet everything was treated as a victory, and the leading celebrant was Auguste.

The amount of energy he devoted to the conquest of the opera public might lead one to think that it was a veritable redoubt of antagonism. Auguste, however, could hardly have asked for a more numerous audience or for one more susceptible to his ministrations. Its size was not matched by its sophistication. Operatic esthetics were of as little concern to most of its members as to Véron himself. Brought up on *vaudeville*, melodrama, and the elaborate spectacles that had been popular on the boulevards since early in the century, this audience "was not interested in art for art's sake. It wanted to be distracted, to be made to forget budgets and bankruptcies. In short, it wanted to be amused; and was ready with its praise and its money for whoever could satisfy that desire." [52] "The public at that time was not blasé, but was eager for pleasures." [53] It was, on the whole, an audience whose acquaintance with the arts was neither long nor profound. Its favorite playwright was Scribe, the inexhaustible portrayer of bourgeois manners in the 19th century. Théodore de Banville observed that its taste in poetry ran to the sentimental romance, while in the graphic arts the colored lithograph was preferred. In opera, likewise, it showed small interest in the classic French traditions and almost as little respect for the great 18th century Italian style.

The fact that the audiences were so untutored in matters of art undoubtedly made them more amenable to the organized persuasion of Auguste. One should not assume, however, that his presence alone was always enough to guarantee the full success of a work. Even he, with all his minions, could not save Cherubini's *Ali-Baba* in 1833, any more than he was able to make Mozart's *Don Giovanni* a popular favorite in 1834. Public taste for the semi-romantic, pseudo-historical operas in the Meyerbeer-Scribe idiom was far too strong at the moment to be sidetracked by any other style, however eminent. Auguste, though, could and did render complete failure less likely or at least less noticeable. By escorting each production with his band of hired applauders he lent a measure of security to the performers, and if necessary, cushioned the effect of any public apathy or disapproval of them or of the work itself.

From the beginning, therefore, the claque had an integral part in Véron's campaign to cement the position of the Opéra as a commercial asset both to himself and to the government. And as a part in the enterprise, the value of Auguste's contribution may be fairly measured by the success of the whole. That, we know, was sensational. Judged by business standards, which are the only ones Véron professed to follow, his tactics, including his consistent and generous use of the claque, were amply justified by their reward at the box office. He amassed a fortune, his associates also reaped a harvest, and the government gained reflected glory from the immense prestige of the Opéra. No one person in that organization is entirely responsible for its success, although much credit must go, of course, to the director himself. Working on the highest level of policy, he was the guiding spirit of the theater. Nevertheless, his own fortune was dependent ultimately upon the effective work done by the lower echelons, in which is included the claque. The latter, under the seasoned leadership of Auguste, not only became, as it were, a trademark of the Opéra, but it earned very early a place as one of the producer's most trusted aids. In Auguste one sees a picturesque figure whose name was a byword in French theatrical circles; and in his trade in claqueurs we find a vivid demonstration of the practical, utilitarian spirit, the professional manner, and the shrewd estimate of effect that characterized French grand opera and made it the most brilliant spectacle of its time.

V

THE *MISE EN SCENE*

THE SPLENDOR of the Opéra after 1830 was no mere dream con-
jured up by a subsidized press, nor was it confined to the dress
of its fashionable audience. The stage itself had a luster which
taxed the descriptive powers of all observers. Véron was not exag-
gerating when he asserted that immense progress had been made in
the "painting, placement, and illumination of the decorations" and
that "the variety and richness of the costumes had never been carried so far" as under his direction.[1]

It was not wasted effort, for the larger part of the public seemed
to have an insatiable appetite for spectacle. This was true at any
level of society and in most theaters. "The habitués of the minor
stages desire above all that their eyes be pleased. We believe," said
Gautier, "there is no example of a melodrama embellished with
decorations, costumes and special lighting which has not returned
at least what it cost." The reason, he felt, was simple. "People are
enamored of the beautiful, the brilliant, and the pompous because
their own existence is shabby, obscure, and miserable." [2] But taste
for the accessories of drama was also strong in the more opulent
world of the great theaters. There too, complained Gustave Planche,
people looked more than they listened. While a few obstinate individuals attempted to catch the first lines of the play, most of the
audience had its eyes turned on the decorations. "When tired of
examining the panels and the furnishings of the room, the aristocracy of the boxes consented to occupy itself with the people on the

stage; but attention was not yet addressed to the actor—only to his costume." The ladies asked themselves anxiously if the dress they saw was not just what they needed for the ball of the following week. "Then they compared the tone of the velvet with the complexion of the actress. The bodice was too long, or perhaps the shoulders were not exposed enough; the coiffure was too high, or it might be that the lower part of the face was too large." Not until the middle of the third act was there really time to find out what the players were saying.[3]

At the Opéra, likewise, a vast amount of attention was concentrated on the settings. The prosperity and popularity of that theater were due, it was said, to the fact that the director understood he must encourage his artists to develop all possible luxury and elegance of scene in the "magical entertainments of this temple."[4] Véron knew as well as Mme. Emile de Girardin that in Paris "an opera, whatever the beauty of its music, cannot be sustained for four acts without ballets and without decorations"; for it was true, unfortunately, that a whole evening could not be devoted to the pleasures of the ear, "especially at the Opéra, where one goes to see and to admire. The public of the Opéra demands that it be dazzled, and the most beautiful singing in the world will never lessen this requirement."[5] "If the Académie Royale de Musique was able with a small number of works to satisfy the curiosity of the public, and alone, among all the theaters of Paris, to enrich itself and remain in favor," the explanation lay in the care and the taste which "presided constantly over all parts of the *mise en scène* in its operas."[6]

A great deal more than just taste, however, went into the creation of the Opéra's stage effects. Talent was present also, and no small amount of real vision. Nothing less could have produced those revolutionary décors which brought the efforts of a century to a climax.

The trend of the day was toward settings that would be realistic and at the same time imaginative in their use of new material devices. The realistic effect was helped by several external improvements such as darkening the house during a performance and lowering the curtain between acts while the scenery was being changed;[7] but of still more importance was the development of a subtler, more varied handling of perspective and light. A greater use was made of real objects, while the ordinary flat backdrop was replaced by one giving the effect of a concave wall on which was painted a panorama designed to be an extension into space of the scene in the foreground.

These changes were part of a movement whose first halting steps were visible as far back as the early decades of the eighteenth century, although the French Opéra then was quite unconcerned with the matter. Quinault's mythological librettos, presenting pictures of gods and goddesses, demi-gods and magicians intervening in the lives of human beings, had no place for such things as realism or local color. In his works the marvelous rather than the ordinary was exploited, and the *mise en scène* derived its character from the supernatural events of the action. The Académie, indeed, during Lully's reign always placed great store upon the mechanical ingenuity displayed in its productions, although in this it merely followed the lead of Italian baroque opera which was first brought to Paris with all its opulence and complex stage machinery by Cardinal Mazarin in the 1640's.

Italian stage designers such as Torelli, Burnacini, and Bibbiena were clearly the masters of the French decorators, but if the art of devising mechanical shows was less perfected in France than in Italy, it was pursued there considerably longer. Italy gradually abandoned the stage machines after 1700 at the time when her librettists began to vary mythology with history and when the virtuoso singer emerged as the chief attraction of the Italian lyric theater, now turned towards the "solo opera"; but France carried on much as before. Fifty years after Lully's death (1687) the works of Rameau continued to give prominence to the apparitions, flights, and metamorphoses of their fabulous characters. These were essential elements of the French lyric drama and they made it the chief refuge of the machinist's skill.

In the second quarter of the eighteenth century the Opéra was paticularly well-fortified in its department of *mise en scène* by the genius of Servandoni (1695–1766), a Florentine architect who was called to Paris in 1724. His contributions to the French stage included a number of brilliant imitations of natural phenomena and a demonstration that décors need not be constructed in the conventionally symmetrical style of the seventeenth century.[8] By varying the perspective and disposing the elements of the scene in a less formal arrangement he gave his compositions something of the "apparent disorder of nature." [9] But though his innovations pointed towards a more individual and realistic type of production, the Opéra did not materially change its ways. The gods and heroes of its fables still wore the wigs, silk stockings and embroidered breeches of the characters in French classical tragedy. The dancers were still masked. Because of its marvelous nature the *tragédie lyrique* was considered much freer than spoken drama, yet it, too, had its traditions. And the prestige of Lully and Quinault was so great that they were maintained in France almost intact until the Revolution.

While the Opéra remained dedicated to displaying the marvels of mythology, the Théâtre-Français was held in the grip of a strong conservative faction which scorned the aid of the decorator's art. Classic French drama in its purest form was a work addressed to the ears and the understanding rather than to the eyes. "The pieces that were performed required a minimum of stage mounting; tragedies or comedies, strictly speaking, could all be played in a common décor." [10] Three traditional sets were used representing the palace, the street and the chamber, and until the middle of the eighteenth century "the play of the actors constituted almost the entire *mise en scène*." [11]

Although the movement for reform made slow progress, this rigidity of scene in the French theater caused unrest among both playwrights and critics throughout the century. In 1722 Houdar de Lamotte (1672–1731) exhorted dramatists to vary their settings and to substitute action and spectacle for narration. Referring to the so-called rule of Aristotle concerning the unity of place which had been codified by Boileau in his *Art Poétique* (1673), Lamotte said: "I would release dramatic authors from the observance of this forced unity which often costs the spectator some events of the play that he should see, and that are now supplied only by narrations less striking than the action itself." [12] Later dissenters from tradition found examples for their arguments in the works of Shakespeare, and a more favorable milieu for stage realism was created by the scientific movement which produced the *Encyclopédie*. Diderot, the guiding spirit of the Encyclopedists, urged an alteration of the elements of spectacle to supplement the new bourgeois tragedy which sought to make dramatic use of the events of daily life.[13] And following his example, authors began to devote particular care to the material execution of their works, making it a point of honor to print in their publications all the necessary indications for their scenic realization. Voltaire composed his tragedies on the older pattern, but welcomed the added attractions provided by his decorator, Brunetti, and encouraged an accuracy of scene and costume [14] which was carried still farther by Beaumarchais. "All that tends to promote truth is precious in a serious drama," wrote the latter. "The dramatist must not permit himself the slightest liberties in regard to the language, habits, or costumes of those he portrays on the stage." [15]

Under the influence of the Opéra, the taste for theatrical display was becoming so great that the drama found it hard to resist its intrusions. A poet need not know the secrets of painting and the mechanics of stage machinery, said Nougaret, "but he must give special attention to the scenic effects in a play and must find means for introducing them properly. Our century," he added, "is greedy for spectacles. A work which rejected them completely would be boring and would soon fail, however touching and sublime it might be. . . . The decorations must be varied; . . . each act should have its own setting." Corneille and Racine did not make use of these accessories, he admitted, and "perhaps their tragedies will always charm the spectators solely by the thought and the beauty of the delivery." But times had changed. "One can say truthfully that the merit of the modern drama depends more on the decorator than on the poet." [16]

Nougaret, who was an advocate of the style of realism proposed by Diderot, spoke forcefully but to no great effect, for the Théâtre-Français was still ruled by the party of Classicism. His efforts and those of other nonconforming spirits of the time merely traced a pattern for the theater; they could not impose it. The decisive break in the ranks of tradition did not occur until after the Revolution. And even then it was forty years before the full effect was seen on the official stages of Paris.

During that time a new theatrical art was born and developed in humbler surroundings. The liberty of scene and the realism of setting which were tentatively sketched by many people in the eighteenth century and which later became so vital in the romantic theater of 1830 were standard elements of the popular stage when Hugo was in his infancy. One finds a complete unfolding of the scenic art of Romanticism in the melodramas produced by Pixérécourt at the Ambigu-Comique and the Gaîté, and in the extraordinary spectacles devised by Baron Taylor and Alaux for the Panorama-Dramatique, by Pierre for the Théâtre-Pittoresque and by Daguerre for his Diorama.

After the Decree of 1791 abolished the monopoly exercised by the royal houses the popular theaters broke forth with an orgy of spectacular entertainments of all kinds. The literary content of most of these was wholly negligible, but that defect was compensated for by the ingenuity and imagination shown in the staging. For a century and a half, wrote Pixérécourt, dramatists had been merely gleaners in the fields of Classicism. "All had been said, and everything had been done." It was necessary, therefore, to invent a new theater distinguished from the old by "the development of those scenic illusions which previously had been neglected and which authors are now constrained to use in order to capture the attention of the popular audience." It was useless, he argued, to spend time on a fine analysis of character for that would not satisfy the people.[17] "The spectacle had become a public institution, a primary necessity like bread." [18]

The catalogue of scenes produced in melodrama from 1789 to 1829 is bewildering in its variety. During the period of the Revolution and early in the nineteenth century these plays were filled with murders and horrors of all kinds perpetrated in suitably ghoulish surroundings and in most cases inspired by the Gothic novels of Anne Radcliffe and Monk Lewis. Decorators specialized in gloomy chateaux, forests, subterranean caverns, old ruins, tombs and abandoned chapels. Later, when this type of melodrama was supplanted by works which drew upon national history and popular tradition, the settings acquired a more natural and realistic tone. Whether concerned with fantasy or history, however, the melodrama was primarily a spectacle, and Pixérécourt was a *metteur en scène* as well as a playwright. As stage manager of the Gaîté, he not only conceived the scenes but made sure that they were properly executed. Along with the other melodramatists he "soon learned the secret of making a poor play a success by skillful advertisement of the elaborate staging." [19] To the romantic opera and drama, this development of the *mise en scène* was probably the most important feature of the popular tragedy. In the opinion of one distinguished scholar "there is no doubt whatsoever that the perfection of the mechanism of the stage in Paris . . . is due in large measure to the work of the melodramatists." [20]

One should not forget, however, the contributions made by the designers of the entertainments known as *spectacles d'optique*. These pictorial shows which had their origin in the panoramas introduced in France in 1787 by the English painter Backer and in 1797 by Robert Fulton, the American, were of various kinds, although they had the common characteristic of being neither drama nor painting.[21] There were no actors, but frequently a commentator was used to explain what was being shown. And instead of acts there were tableaux. Specializing in the panoramic treatment of scenes, the artists reproduced picturesque sites and monuments and the most complex natural phenomena with an accuracy that amazed everyone. At M. Pierre's Théâtre-Pittoresque "one sees in miniature the grandest spectacles of nature." Everything, we are told, was done there much better than at the Opéra. "The rising and setting of the sun are more beautiful; nature is better imitated; the gardens and groves are fresher; the streets, bridges, public places, temples, and monuments are represented with the greatest exactness." [22]

The scope of popular spectacle was extended even further by Louis Daguerre (1789–1851). Remembered by us yet as the inventor of the photographic process bearing his name, he first became known for his work in the theater. Beginning his career at the Ambigu-Comique, he created décors which won success for a vast number of melodramas, pantomimes, and ballets. Panoramic effects particularly excited his fancy for he was constantly occupied with enlarging the horizon of the stage. "It appears that Daguerre deserves the principal credit for introducing open and continuous tableaux in place of the flat scenes formerly used." [23] "No one carried as far as he the art of captivating the eyes by the cunning use of perspective. His brush was especially gifted in the depiction of misty landscapes, nocturnal effects, awesome scenes of nature, and stately ruins." [24]

To the remarkable effects of perspective that he achieved in his early panoramas Daguerre later added a revolutionary display of stage lighting. The introduction of gas in the theater replacing the Argand lamps [25] formerly used opened up a whole new field of opportunity to the decorators, and he again was one of the first to exploit it in his invention called the "Diorama." Shown in a circular room seating about 350 people, this was a species of painting, partly opaque and partly transparent, which depended for its effects of illusion on the play of light and color. "At each change of view the movable floor turned, and with it all the spectators, who thus were carried without disturbance before a series of marvelously effective tableaux." [26] Needless to say, "the Diorama excited universal curiosity and obtained the approbation of all artists and men of taste." [27]

Gautier could well report that "the time of the purely visual spectacle had arrived." [28] Despite the restrictions imposed on them by Napoleon and the Restoration Governments, the popular theaters flourished; and each attempted to outdo the other in the lavishness and ingenuity of its décors and costumes. The demand for spectacle was apparently insatiable. Indeed, it was so great that finally even the staid Théâtre-Français was forced to yield to the pressure of public taste. Baron Taylor, the former decorator and director of the Panorama-Dramatique, was appointed Royal Commissioner of the state theater in 1825, and within a few months a change was visible in its productions.

Pichat's tragedy, *Léonidas,* was the first work to feel the hand of the Commissioner. Mounted in original settings designed by Taylor, it "introduced in the Rue de Richelieu, under the shield of an old-fashioned tragedy new ideas of local color and of historical fidelity." [29] When the piece was performed on November 27, 1825, all agreed they "had never seen at the Théâtre-Français anything to match the decorations, the costumes and the *mise en scène.* Cries and stamping of feet greeted the rise of the curtain for each act." [30] The evening was a success, not merely for Pichat who is unimportant, but for the theatrical methods of the Boulevard which had finally broken into the conservative stronghold and which were soon to be incorporated into the romantic statement of belief.

The province of drama is the real, said Hugo in the Preface to *Cromwell*. If one follows the old rule concerning the unity of place, "all that is too characteristic, too intimate, too localized, to occur in the anteroom or in the public square . . . takes place off the stage. We see in the theater, as it were, only the points of the action. . . . In place of scenes we have narrations, for tableaux we are given descriptions." However, he added, it is now being understood that dramatic reality can only be expressed in an exact setting. "The speaking or acting characters are not the sole means for engraving a faithful impression of events on the mind of the spectator." The place of the action becomes itself a powerful witness to the nature of the drama. The theater is a mirror. "All that exists in the world, in history, in life, in man must and can be reflected there." In the names of nature and truth, every resource must be used to attain the maximum scenic illusion.

Romanticism thus condemned unequivocally the scenic restraint of the classical theater. *Cromwell* itself, paradoxically, was unplayable, but its preface was the proclamation of liberty for the stage. Sanctioned by Hugo, the art of spectacle then received its *droit de cité* at the Théâtre-Français with the production on February 10, 1829 of Alexandre Dumas' *Henri III et sa cour*. "For the first time," said one of the decorators, "we were permitted to transport the spectators to the period in which the action takes place, and to show the historical characters framed in a *mise en scène* conforming absolutely to reality." [31] The historical genre in the manner of the popular theaters was confirmed. Henceforth, there was a constant demand for new décors and novel effects of all kinds. "The palette of the decorator gained remarkably in power," [32] and painters and designers found themselves raised to a commanding position in any production at the Théâtre-Français.

Turning back a year we find that a similar development took place at the Académie Royale de Musique. And we may note further that here, too, it came after a long period of almost complete prostration. For a generation the lyric theater, like its sister stage in the Rue de Richelieu, had been afflicted with a paralysis in all its members. Accustomed as we are to think of the Parisian Opéra in the nineteenth century as the ultimate home of illusion, the hatching ground of anything new in spectacle, it is difficult to realize how far it had sunk from its earlier state of eminence in this field. Yet that it had fallen is hardly open to doubt. If the singing was poor, the décors were no less inadequate. While it was still argued that the lyric drama was "in part a spectacle for the eyes," [33] by 1827 the *mise en scène* was said to be "the most neglected branch of the opera. . . . In its present state it ruins the impression of all the other elements." [34] Content to "trudge along in the old rut, producing nothing and inventing nothing," the Opéra was "far behind the theaters of the Boulevard in the art of preparing its effects." [35]

To be sure, there had been occasional bursts of activity during the Restoration period, but these were quite isolated. Nicolo's work entitled, *Aladin ou la Lampe Merveilleuse*, which, appropriately enough, marked the first use of gas lighting in the Académie, received an ovation in 1822 because of its unusual décors. But no consistent effort was made to take advantage of the new techniques of stage production until a committee was appointed by the Maison du Roi in 1827 to suggest improvements in the *mise en scène* of the Opéra.

Since Edmond Duponchel, who became director of the Académie after Véron, was the most active member of this group, results were soon forthcoming. A student of architecture who also dabbled in archeology, Duponchel was interested above all in the theater. His knowledge of literature and music was limited, but not his talent as a stage designer. Known later as the "Alexander of the *mise en scène*," he "was an artist, an inventor of decorative effects who had an innate passion for magnificent settings." [36] Unmoved by the demands of singers and dancers, his mind was fixed on the beauties of the scene. This "lean, yellowish, pale man . . . of distinguished appearance . . . who looked as if he were in perpetual mourning," [37] was a partisan of all the new tendencies in theatrical design. Not content simply to ameliorate the unhappy condition in which he found the Opéra, he set himself the task of modernizing its stage completely.

Duponchel's aide in this endeavor was Pierre Cicéri (1782–1868), in his day perhaps the most famous man on the roster of the royal theaters. As a youth he was greatly interested in music, and at the age of seventeen entered the Conservatoire with the intention of becoming a professional singer. His hopes were dashed, however, after several years of study, when he was rendered lame in a carriage accident. Before then he had amused himself by sketching in his leisure hours, but from that time he devoted himself completely to the arts of painting and design. In 1809 he was engaged to paint landscapes for the Opéra and in 1810 was named decorator-in-chief. Thereafter, his career during the next twenty years was at once a story of personal success and a summary of the course taken by the lyric theater.

He began his work as an academician doing stilted landscapes in the pompous, unrealistic style of the *Ancien Régime*, and for some time he remained on the beaten track of Classicism.[38] He could not fail, though, to see what was being done in the popular theaters, and since his mind was not irrevocably dedicated to the classical ideal, he was willing to learn from the decorators of the Boulevard. He was also willing to work in the secondary theaters. While his official position required him to furnish décors for both the Opéra and the Théâtre-Français, he found time to extend his activities to the Panorama-Dramatique, the Porte Saint-Martin, the Nouveautés and even to the equestrian shows at the Cirque-Olympique.[39] This experience, which brought him in contact particularly with the productions and the ideas of Baron Taylor and Daguerre, was enough to pull him completely into the progressive camp.

If the principles of popular decoration were not applied more extensively in the Opéra before 1828 it was due to no fault of his. "Decorators such as Cicéri or Daguerre could have done more had they been supported"; but La Rochefoucauld, the Superintendent of Theaters in Paris, was indifferent to their plans. "The *mise en scène* was a dead letter to him." [40] Not until Duponchel was delegated to improve the Opéra productions did Cicéri have an opportunity to demonstrate in full the revolutionary technique he had acquired in his association with the secondary theaters.

The opera which brought the talents of Duponchel and Cicéri together for the first time was Auber's *La Muette de Portici* (1828), a piece which was unique in a number of ways. It introduced Scribe to the Opéra; by presenting a vivid picture of Neapolitan life, it became the first of the grand opera line in France to make much of the Romantic's interest in local color; and it marked the first complete exhibition in the Rue le Peletier of nineteenth-century stage design. *La Muette* "constituted a revolution in the practice of *mise en scène* at the Opéra because of the special and novel study that had been made of the costumes and accessories." [41] There was much admiration for the scene representing a beach on the Mediterranean and for the palace of the Spanish Viceroy with its massive stone staircase rising to a terrace which overlooked Vesuvius in the distance; but the real tour de force was the final view showing the volcano in action. In preparation for it, Cicéri was even sent by the Government to study the effects created in Pacini's *L'Ultimo Giorno di Pompeia* (1827) at the La Scala Opera in Milan. Neither time nor money were wasted, for the scene became the most celebrated in Paris. The eruption of Vesuvius was a popular theme on the Boulevard and had been presented already by Daguerre's Diorama and several other theaters; but it was generally agreed that the Duponchel-Cicéri spectacle surpassed all others. "The Opéra never mounted a work more carefully in respect to the *mise en scène*, ballets, decorations and costumes. Truth was especially sought, and it must be admitted that nothing was neglected to attain this goal." [42]

Following this extraordinary achievement, Cicéri experimented in *La Belle au bois dormant* (1829) with a mobile panorama, "a shifting decoration which caused a delightful perspective to unfold before the undulations of a boat." [43] And later in the same year he and his associates also created several striking pictures of the Swiss landscape in Rossini's *Guillaume Tell* (1829). Nothing really comparable, however, to the scenic wonders of *La Muette* was produced at the Opéra again until the advent of Véron. Given the unstinted support of this administrator, the decorators then came fully into their own. Their fondest dreams were realized, and after 1831, it was said, "the Opéra furnished models of stagecraft which have never been surpassed." [44]

Robert le Diable, Véron's first large-scale production, set the tone for his whole administration. No effort was spared in the endeavor to make this opera a visual masterpiece. The English stagetraps were introduced, gas illumination was used for the first time on the French opera stage and advantage was taken of the varied effects of perspective, illusion and chiaroscuro which had been developed in the Boulevard theaters. The settings were new and they were also expensive. "The costumes are of the utmost richness; . . . and the staging does great honor to M. Duponchel. We are assured that the *mise en scène* of this opera cost nearly 200,000 francs; but it is money well spent. For a long while it was considered impossible to give more pomp and luxury to the Opéra; M. Véron has proved the contrary." [45]

Nothing could be better calculated to stir the imagination of men like Duponchel and Cicéri than the story of *Robert* with all its "medieval" pageantry and extravagant mummery. It offered opportunity both for historical reproductions and for the wildest play of fancy. There were pleasures for the eye from the opening tableau presenting an animated picture of medieval knighthood to the final disappearance of Bertram in a cloud of fire and brimstone. Each part of the work was given its own individual coloring, but a fair idea of the general scope and style of the decorations may be gained from the famous cloister scene of the third act. It was described by the *Revue des Deux Mondes* in this way: "We are in an abandoned monastery. The walls fall in ruins. The silent tombs are filled with white statues. Mysterious rays of the moon illuminate the melancholy interior with their pale light. Suddenly music is heard . . . and the immobile statues come to life. A throng of silent shadows glides through the arches. All the women discard their nun's costumes. They shake off the cold dust of the tombs and immediately return to the delights of their former life. They dance like bacchantes, they gambol like lords, they drink like soldiers." [46]

No contemporary account fails to pay its respects to this particular triumph of the decorator's art; yet it reached its ultimate state only by scrapping the original ideas of Meyerbeer and Scribe.

Oddly enough, they suggested having the pantomime and dance unfold in the usual operatic Olympus, furnished on the standard pattern with a "superannuated apparatus of quivers, arrows, gauze and Cupids." Duponchel, however, was properly horrified at such a plan and soon succeeded in convincing his colleagues and Véron of the ridiculousness of these classical fripperies.[47] Instead then of a stereotyped décor wholly at variance with the popular character of the legend, the artists designed a scene that in spirit came straight from the world of the Boulevard. Moreover, due especially to Duponchel's training and proclivities, the setting was given an architectural form which pretended to some historical accuracy. The stage became a lofty, vaulted gallery divided by arches resting on columns and opening on a burial ground. It was said to be a reproduction of an existing sixteenth-century monument: the cloister of Montfort-l'Amaury, whose sepulchral atmosphere was evoked by Hugo in one of his early odes.[48]

Interest in the medieval period—or in what passed for it—which had been mounting in the French theater for many years, reached a peak at this time. Séchan, a student and colleague of Cicéri, said that for those at the Opéra the Middle Ages became "the true artistic school. We studied them with an unreflecting passion—the costumes, the architecture, down to the smallest details of the furniture." Like the public, decorators were fascinated by the general term "medieval," but they were concerned also to give it some specific content. The study of local color had become a necessity in the theater. The time was past when the most diverse places could be indifferently represented. "It was desired now that the characters of each piece should be shown in their true costumes and in the actual surroundings where they had lived."[49]

Sporadic attempts had been made before to bring the opera stage abreast of its time, and in *La Muette de Portici* a notable success in this respect had been achieved. The revolution begun there was clinched with the production of *Robert le Diable*. "At last we have something new," said *Le Constitutionnel*. No longer must one suffer with the "ancient palaces disturbed by the last glimmerings of a dying Argand lamp, or with the antique relics and the flimsy columns which tremble at the slightest touch of a Venus in curl-papers or of a Cupid in pumps." [50] There was no turning back from this point even if Véron had wished to do so. The public had seen what could be done at the Opéra and would not be satisfied with anything less. The productions of *La Muette* and *Robert* became the standards by which other works were judged. Henceforth, the director "was obliged to go to enormous expense for the *mise en scène* of the slightest work that he consented to put in rehearsal." [51]

Since elaborate settings were in such demand it was a matter of clear necessity to find scripts that permitted the full exercise of the decorator's talents, and the obvious place to go for such books was the popular theater. The playwrights of the Boulevard were not masters of language, but they did appreciate the commercial value of spectacle. It was to this source, then, that Véron turned; and in Scribe he found a man perfectly suited to himself and to the requirements of grand opera. Every new libretto that Véron used came from this writer's facile pen, and not one of them failed to present adequate openings for the work of Duponchel and Cicéri.

Auber's *Le Serment ou Les Faux Monnayeurs*, given on October 1, 1832, included scenes in its three acts showing the interior of an inn, a Gothic chamber, and a busy street where merchants of all races dressed in native costumes peddled their wares. The four-act opera by Cherubini entitled *Ali-Baba ou Les Quarante Voleurs* (1833) was still more colorful and varied. "The costumes display a richness and fidelity which do the greatest honor to the talents of M. Duponchel. If the decorations are not as brilliant as those in *Robert* . . . they are noteworthy for the skill with which the effects of nature are reproduced, as in the forest scene and in the cave of the robbers." The work's greatest spectacle, however, was Ali-Baba's vast bazaar filled with all manner of rich merchandise. Here, "one was transported completely to the Orient." [52]

These minor pieces aroused a certain amount of interest, but their settings could not be compared to the splendid décors of *Gustave III* (1833) and *La Juive* (1835). The latter works, whose scores were written by Auber and Halévy respectively, maintained in every way the high scenic level established by *Robert*. The opening curtain of Auber's opera "rises on the magnificent waiting room of the palace at Stockholm which Gustave III had constructed on the model of the great hall of Versailles. One is already struck with astonishment at this first tableau. Recall the immense, marble salon of Versailles, embellished with busts and statues, its ceilings ornamented with gilded carvings, all in a grand style at once heavy, majestic, and severe. All of this sumptuous dwelling is transferred to the stage with unbelievable exactness. It is so accurate that the French Ambassador to Sweden who was sitting near us said that for a moment he thought he had returned to his post." [53]

From this auspicious beginning the opera proceeded on its way to the famous ball scene of the fifth act. "The stage represents an immense gallery terminating in a playhouse. The boxes and the balconies are occupied by courtiers and courtesans, the parquet is filled with maskers of every description. . . . One is dazzled by the movement and gaiety when this army of mountebanks . . . joins in the dance. . . . The beauty of the décor flooded by the light of sixty chandeliers, the freshness and richness of the costumes, the brilliance of the colors . . . all form an enchanting picture." [54] "It was like an Arabian tale. . . . The imagination had never before dreamed its equal." [55] "When the curtain arose on this prodigious scene in *Gustave,* boxes, orchestra, stalls, and parterre burst forth with shouts of admiration that lasted throughout the ballet." [56]

While the merit of *Gustave III* rests almost entirely on the splendor of its finale, *La Juive* is a much more substantial musicodramatic work. In the story of the young Jewess and her Christian lover there is no apparent need for the pretentious décors, fanciful lighting, trap doors, and other paraphernalia so dear to the boulevardier of the early 1800's. The events in themselves do not cry for elaborate staging. They might conceivably have been played in quite simple sets, placing the emphasis entirely upon the double tragedy of infidelity and religious intolerance. That they were not treated so, however, is hardly surprising in view of the road that French opera was taking at the time. To Véron and his decorators it would have been unthinkable to neglect the many possibilities for spectacle connected with the period and setting of the play. The period was the early part of the fifteenth century at the time when three Popes were wrangling over the Holy See. The place was Constance where a Council had been summoned by John XXIII and the Emperor Sigismund to end the great schism dividing the Occident. It was an occasion, obviously, for a large amount of pomp and ceremony—enough to challenge the imagination and ingenuity of the complete staff at the opera house. The five immense décors planned for *La Juive* furnished work for everyone. A host of supernumeraries was enlisted, and it was even necessary to requisition the horses of Franconi's Cirque-Olympique.

For pure spectacle the two scenes that aroused the most enthusiasm in contemporary audiences were the cortège of secular and ecclesiastical dignitaries at the end of the first act and the festival in act three celebrating the return of a conquering Prince. The first of these was described as follows: "The cortège advances . . . , the Imperial troops marching past the portals of the Cathedral. Princes of the Church precede the Emperor. Cardinal Brogni is seated under a magnificent canopy. . . . At the appearance of Sigismund and the officials of the Empire, all on horseback, the bells of the Cathedral and of other churches in the city are rung, and the sound of cannon is heard." [57] In the opinion of *Le Courrier Français,* this procession should be considered the eighth wonder of the world. "Nothing is missing in this prodigious resurrection of a distant century. The costumes of the warriors, civilians and ecclesiastics are not imitated but reproduced to the smallest details. The armor is no longer pasteboard; it is made of real metal. One sees men of iron, men of silver, men of gold! The Emperor Sigismund, for instance, is a glittering ingot from head to foot. The horses, not less historically outfitted than their riders, prance and turn . . . the procession stretches without end. In truth, if one is not careful, the Opéra will become a power capable of throwing its armies into the balance of Europe." [58]

The same journal called the grand festival "one of the most beautiful spectacles of nature. In the foreground one sees sumptuous gardens, back of them is a ravishing landscape, and still farther in the background is the pure and resplendent majesty of Lake Constance. The festival is a twin sister of the cortège; there is the same prodigality in the skillful resurrection of the past. The Emperor Sigismund presides at the banquet, served by four mounted Electors, following the formal text of the Golden Bull. The interlude . . . without which there could be no royal banquet, is not forgotten. An enchanted tower appears. Knights besiege it and suddenly each bastion of the tower is changed into a cell housing a nymph who begins to dance as one assuredly did not dance in the Middle Ages. . . ." [59]

"The Middle Ages in their entirety are unfolded before us," said Gautier. "One sees ecclesiastical and feudal ceremonies, townsmen proud of their guilds, magnificent Cardinals, knights banneret, glittering crests, bejeweled mitres, birettas the color of blood, . . . heralds, caparisoned, neighing chargers, crowds of peasants, clusters of noblemen, ladies in flowing robes, Capuchin friars. . . . It is the medieval period itself in all the infinite variety of its dress and its hierarchy." [60] "The magnificence of the costumes and décors surpassed all expectations." [61] "One should see this great work at least ten times to understand and savor it completely." [62]

La Juive undoubtedly marked the apex in the art of the *metteurs en scène* at the Opéra. Beyond this it was hardly possible to go and still leave any room for drama and music. A great many people, indeed, thought that the claims of spectacle both in spoken drama and in opera had already been pushed much too far. The creation of what amounted to a new power in the theater, threatening to override the rights of poet, actor, composer and singer, was bound to cause misgivings if not open hostility in some quarters. After the success of *Henri III* the writers of the old school addressed a petition to the King begging him to come to the rescue of the drama. The Romanticists, they insisted, were ruining the theater "to satisfy the requirements of this genre, whose aim is less to elevate the spirit and touch the heart than to dazzle the eyes by material means, by the show of decorations, and by the brilliance of the spectacle." [63] The modern stage is ruled by its accessories, exclaimed Jules Janin.[64] "The application of the scenic methods which, at the moment, appeared to save the languishing art of drama, has been disastrous." Drama became only a pretext for the decorations as a result of proclaiming the "primordial importance of the exact locality" of the action, and of bestowing "more care on the dress of the hero than on his character." [65] "Public pleasures as well as private," said Louis de Bonald, "may cause ruin by their excess; and perhaps we are not far from the time when the spectacle in France will kill the art of the theater." [66]

Connoisseurs of the opera were equally worried. "Where are we heading," asked the painter Delacroix, "that so much foreign aid must be given to music, the mightiest of the arts, to poetry, which should be bound to music alone, and to declamation, gesture, and song, which give force to all the other arts?" [67] The opera, answered Castil-Blaze, was moving in the direction the audiences wished. What else could be expected "in a country where people do not care for music"? [68] They will be satisfied only if given "spectacle sufficient to their needs, and to their poetico-musical intelligence which is still obtuse and nebulous." [69] French opera, he added, was the "most sumptuous and ridiculous spectacle in the world." It was a "ravishing, delicious exhibition for the young, the deaf, and the ignorant." [70] It achieved success because "the Parisian public judged music by the décors, the costumes, the richly ornamented horses, the velvet, the satin, the armor, and all the luxury of the setting. Neglect these pompous accessories and the talent of the musician would be lost on an assembly wonderfully incapable of appreciating it." [71]

Nourrit was also disheartened by the course of the Opéra, but kept his faith in public understanding, feeling that the fault lay rather with an administration which occupied itself much more with the *mise en scène* than with the artists and authors. "The decorator, the furbisher, the metalsmith, the jeweller, the embroiderer, the upholsterer . . . are today the men of art engaged by M. Véron for the service of the Opéra. Poetry, music, song, and dance are only the pretexts to set off his prodigalities." [72]

Other critics less bitter in tone were just as aware of what was happening. Scudo, for instance, regretted that "the accessory has become the principal element, and that truth of feeling has been displaced by exactness of costumes and décors." [73] Even the usually sympathetic *L'Artiste* cautioned Duponchel on the retirement of Véron not to forget that "the Opéra is above all a musical institution. . . . All the seductions of painting, all the illusions of the *mise en scène,* must serve music as a splendid and harmonious entourage, but must not seek to efface it." [74]

Gautier, however, stepped outside the chorus of condemnation.

He recognized that the decorator's power in the theater of his day was immense, and was a bit awed by this "vast, profound, complex art" that he saw. In his eyes, the *metteur en scène* was something of a wonder-worker who of necessity must be a veritable storehouse of information. He was a man, the critic said, who understood perspective in a "rigorous, geometrical, absolute fashion. He was skilled in the projection of light and shadow, he designed buildings as well as an architect, he proceeded in a completely scientific manner to draft and dispose his décors. . . . But this was only the material part of his work. In order to satisfy the unforeseen demands of authors, he must possess a thorough knowledge of all countries, all periods and all styles." [75]

Out of his respect for the decorator, Gautier reminded the Théâtre-Italien that "perfection of the musical execution does not exempt one from taking great pains with the material and visible part of the drama. Without that, opera becomes a concert." [76] Accepting the audiences more or less on their own terms, he observed that "we are no longer living at a time when the inscription— 'magnificent palace'—nailed to a post, suffices for the illusion of the spectators." Shakespeare may have demanded nothing more, but "we bourgeois . . . have a somewhat sluggish imagination and are essentially lacking in naïveté." [77]

As this last statement tacitly admitted, the reforms and expansion of stage decoration were there to stay. Adverse criticism of them and of their practitioners was undoubtedly justified in many respects, but it was unavailing. The *metteur en scène* had won his spurs in France at a time when dramatic production was weak, and he had become so strongly entrenched that he was not to be easily demoted.

His influence was of such importance that an adequate impression of theatrical art in 1830 is impossible without considering its realization on the stage. The English music critic, Chorley, wrote that it is necessary to "see Meyerbeer's operas as well as hear them, and at the Académie Royale. . . . All arrangements and transcripts of them have but a value in proportion as fancy is pliant and willing to call up all the pride, pomp and circumstance which belong to their representation in Paris." [78] One may add that these operas should be seen not only for the sheer splendor of their production, but because the scenery had become an integral part of the whole composition. It had ceased to be merely an adjunct to drama and music, and had now begun to exercise a real, formative influence on these arts.

That control, noticeable from the moment the new style of *mise en scène* was introduced at the Opéra, arose out of the organization of the décors into tableaux. As the scene itself gained extension, magnificence, and specific content it drew the other elements of the lyric theater into its orbit. The first result was that music and drama took on the spectacular character of the settings, but the second and more important consequence was that they tended also to assume a formal shape which in essentials was a complement of the décors. The massive, colorful tableaux that were conceived in the popular theater as purely visual spectacles were transferred to the Opéra where they were clothed in music and given dramatic substance. A grand opera of the 1830's thus was less a musical drama in five acts than a musico-dramatic spectacle in so many tableaux. On that pattern Scribe wrote his librettos and Meyerbeer composed his scores.

VI

SCRIBE, THE LIBRETTIST

I N THE ensemble of men who joined to produce French grand opera it was the union of talents which ultimately gave the form its unique character and which insured its complete success. Yet it is also true that in this concert of effort certain individual contributions stand forth as props for the whole enterprise. Of particular importance in this respect is the work of Scribe, for it was he in large measure who made grand opera possible by channeling the brilliant scenic innovations of Cicéri and Duponchel into a clear dramatic structure designed to challenge the eye, appeal to the contemporary mind, and satisfy the musical requirements of the composer.

This was something new that came to the Opéra—both new and exceedingly far-reaching in its effect. Yet it was created by Scribe merely as part of the day's work. Novelty was nothing unusual with him, for he remade every dramatic genre that he touched. Opera was simply the last species in a long line to feel the rejuvenating effect of his hand.

Wherever he went, the stage flourished. It may be said of him as of his great contemporary, Alexandre Dumas, that "he was not only a man of the theater, but the incarnation of the theater." [1] "He lived, moved, and had his being in things theatrical." [2] Born in 1791 of a moderately successful Parisian silk merchant, Scribe began his public career when he was twenty. After making a brilliant scholastic record at Sainte-Barbe he followed his mother's wish and studied law, receiving his degree in 1815. However, even while attending law school he was seldom without a play in his pocket and apparently never without several in his head. Beginning as a writer of *vaudevilles,* he first reached the stage in 1811 with the production of *Les Dervis* at the Théâtre du Vaudeville. The next few years were marked more by persistence than success, but in 1815 *Une Nuit de la Garde Nationale* started him on the series of *comédies-vaudevilles* dealing with characters and manners in Restoration society which made him the most sought-after author in the Boulevard theaters. In 1821 he had fourteen plays produced successfully, and between 1820 and 1830 at the Gymnase no less than one hundred of his pieces were given. During this period he also invaded the Théâtre-Français and established himself at the Théâtre de l'Opéra-Comique. *Valérie* in 1816 and *Le Mariage d'Argent* in 1827 brought him to France's first stage, although his position there was insecure until *Bertrand et Raton* was given in 1833. At the Opéra-Comique he made six attempts dating from 1813 before *La Neige* (1823) and *La Dame Blanche* (1825), by their vivacity and *élan,* roused that theater from the slump it had experienced following the great days of Duni (1709–1775), Philidor (1726–1795), Monsigny (1729–1817), and Grétry (1742–1813), and settled his position as the foremost librettist in Paris. Outside the Théâtre-Italien, the Opéra then was the only important stage remaining in the city which had not felt the influence of Scribe, and that oversight was remedied with the production of *La Muette de Portici* in 1828.

The transformation effected by Scribe in the musical theater was thus foreshadowed by his earlier work in the spoken drama. In each case, both technique and substance were modified. Gifted as much as any other writer of the nineteenth century with a sense for theatrical effect, he was able almost from the beginning to put his material into forms that are at once ingenious and clear and always eminently playable. Unlike those who take to the theater for its glamor or because it is fashionable, Scribe went there from necessity. The dramatic form was his only avenue of expression. Whatever he saw or thought appeared to him through the optics of the playhouse. In the jargon of today, his theater was truly "functional" since it grew completely out of the needs and the possibilities of the stage itself. Allowing for the presence of music which necessarily calls for a simpler, less wordy play, the opera librettos of Scribe demonstrate much the same clear and dextrous treatment of material that we see in his *vaudevilles* and comedies. The *péripéties* of the action in the latter are more involved—although the third act of *Les Huguenots* may appear to disprove this—but the opera benefited quite as much as the drama from his unrivalled skill in handling difficult plots and from his ability to turn a situation so that it showed up to the best advantage in front of the foolights.

While Scribe's great technical facility has become almost legendary, however, we often tend to forget that his service to the theater is not restricted merely to a demonstration of how to keep a complicated plot under control. Of at least equal importance are the changes he introduced in the dramatic material itself. Here again, both the spoken and the lyric drama were the beneficiaries of his innovations. To the one he gave the actualities of contemporary life and to the other he brought the historical frame and the broad social questions debated by liberal romanticists.

Finding *vaudeville* almost smothered in the faded costumes, sets, and other impedimenta of eighteenth-century convention, he resolved, in his own words, to make the stage a reflection of his time; [3] and to this end he peopled it with the shopkeepers and clerks, the brokers, bankers, lawyers, and doctors who formed the great middle class that ruled France in the nineteenth century during the ascendancy of the bourgeoisie. Thus, through the medium of *vaudeville*, France's age-old combination of song and satire, Scribe brought to conclusion the eighteenth century's futile attempts to break down the classical restrictions which kept the stage at a distance from the events and people of ordinary life. Earlier variants like the *comédies larmoyantes* of Nivelle de la Chaussée (1692–1754) and the *drame bourgeois* of Diderot (1713–1784) had been created to bridge the gap between convention and reality, but these efforts were premature. The movement towards a more localized kind of theater was insubstantial and doomed to failure until the Revolution dissolved the ancient hierarchical organization of society and made a similar breach in the bonds of the dramatic genres. As social barriers were relaxed, so the distinctions of the theatrical species melted; and in the newly-found freedom the individual emerged, made his way to the stage and brought with him the settings and the customs of the society from which he came.

In giving us a running account of Parisian bourgeois life, Scribe, unlike most of the romantic playwrights, "simply renewed the traditions of dramatic art. The drama of Victor Hugo, however magnificently it soars, marked an interruption in the development of the *théâtre d'observation* . . . all the confused aspirations, all the obscure tendencies, all the more or less lucid theories of Sedaine, Diderot, and Beaumarchais converged in Scribe who immediately gave them a definitive form. He solved the problem of the "contemporary" piece, which . . . his predecessors had perceived only dimly. He went beyond the comedy of character and led the way to the comedy of manners." [4]

As a trail blazer, however, Scribe continued as he began: a bourgeois. He never deviated from the principles of his class, since he wrote primarily about and for the bourgeoisie, who formed, next to the peasants, the largest group in French society by 1830. Their desires and their morality were his, and their thoughts were distilled through his brain. All the prudence and the prudery of nineteenth century bourgeois life found their apology and their expression in the pages of his works.

Scribe never cultivated eccentricities of dress or behavior, although "it was the fashion in the romantic school for a man to be wan, livid, greenish, and somewhat cadaverous, if possible, for thus did one attain the fateful Byronic, Giaour look of a person devoured by passion and remorse." [5] On him the *mal du siècle* had no hold. The sorrows of Werther or of René were as foreign to his practical, workaday nature as they were to the robust spirit of Alexandre Dumas. In particular, of course, he avoided the manner of those who, "though in reality the best of fellows, loved to look like grim ruffians, if only to instil wholesome fear in the breasts of the bourgeoisie." [6] All of the more picturesque exercises of individuality were shunned by him because he was first, last, and always, the indefatigable worker and exemplar of the writer who makes of his art a popular expression and a substantial means of livelihood. He was primarily an artisan, a play-carpenter if you will, who utilized his talents for the stage as another might exploit a gold mine.

Scribe was not, and made no pretense of being, a profound thinker. In his plays he seldom ventured beyond questions of everyday life relating generally to money or the home. Marriage and the dowry, legacies, bankruptcies, and financial speculations were the usual topics of discussion. Honest effort and conservative middle-class morality received the accolade of approval. Yet with all his devotion to the mundane affairs of the "solid" citizen, he proved in his opera librettos that he was not so immersed in the problems of the parvenu that he was completely unaware of the larger issues of contemporary thought. The boldest subjects of political and religious freedom were touched on in works like *La Muette de Portici* (1828), *La Juive* (1835), and *Les Huguenots* (1836); and to this extent Scribe opened the Opéra to the current of liberal, anti-clerical ideas which ran through Romanticism after 1830.

At first glance, Scribe's opera libretti may seem to have a somewhat freerer intellectual tone than is commonly associated with the bourgeoisie, but the disparity is more apparent than real. As a matter of fact, these pieces represent quite faithfully the attitudes of that class. Scribe did not forget that the Revolution of 1830 got its impulse from a liberal middle class which could stomach neither the despotism nor the incipient theocracy of Charles X's reign. He also knew, though, that the bourgeoisie were not a class of professional reformers or philosophers. Liberalism was the very sun of their existence, but for everyday life its pure rays were too bright. They had to be filtered through a screen of custom and practical expediency.

So it was that with the liberal elements of his libretti there was always added a sufficient leavening of operatic tradition and bourgeois intellectual convention to keep the pieces within the boundaries of the middle class public for which he wrote. Scribe in his own person was the complete expression of bourgeois thought and manners. If he often displayed a lack of taste and appeared as a vulgarizer of Romanticism, the faults were shared by his public and indeed served to attract rather than to alienate contemporary audiences. He succeeded so well because he kept to their level, because he gave the bourgeoisie the judicious mixture of pleasure and idealism that they wanted and did so without making excessive demands upon either their intelligence or their imagination.

Forward looking in some respects while consciously circumscribed in others, Scribe's works exemplify that combination of novelty and convention which is always profitable in the theater. It is obvious they do not stand for an advanced type of the Romanticism defined by Hugo as "liberalism in art." [7] They represent, nevertheless, the attitude of the majority of people in Scribe's day, and to some extent they reflect also the path taken by the embattled minorities actively engaged in the dispute about Romanticism.

We read of the great struggle over *Hernani* [8] and it may seem that in 1830 all men were either completely for or against Romanticism. Such a view, however, seriously distorts the history of the early nineteenth century and creates a hard and fast dichotomy of romanticists and non-romanticists which is much too rigid to be true. In the theater as elsewhere one finds even the leaders of the opposing camps making concessions to the claims of their rivals. Hugo, the acknowledged legislator of Romanticism, demonstrated his traditional ties as he charged forth with *Hernani,* the revolutionary drama which turned out to be in form a tragic romance in five acts and in verse. Dumas, likewise, in *Christine* (1830), *Charles VII chez ses grands vassaux* (1831), and *Caligula* (1837), bowed to the weight of classical authority by casting these works in the usual mold of French tragic drama. And on the other side, Casimir Delavigne (1793–1843), the most popular of the pseudo-classical dramatists, signalized in *Marino Faliero* (1829) and *Louis XI* (1832) the belated attempt by the conservative party to accommodate the form of tragedy to the modern spirit and taste.

In 1830, therefore, there was compromise in art as well as in politics. All kinds of dramatists—romanticists, pseudo-classicists and the myriad popular writers who shifted with the winds of fashion—made their collective and individual concessions to the opposing claims. One must not assume, however, that the balance between Classicism and Romanticism was kept in any way equal. The incoming tide of Romanticism was too powerful and pervasive for that. The Théâtre-Français, as a contemporary critic said, "was invaded on all sides by the parodists of Shakespeare and Schiller. . . . There was room for plays from every theater in Europe, but none for the works of Molière, Racine, Corneille or their imitators." [9] Conciliation with the newer doctrines was the only course left to conservative dramatists who wished their plays to reach the stage. Classicism, or rather pseudo-classicism—for the work of men like Népomucène Lemercier (1771–1840) and Casimir Delavigne bears to the seventeenth century style only the resemblance of a pallid copy—still served as a somewhat insecure platform for a small, ineffectual minority; but those remaining adherents were forced to adopt at least some of the outward features of Romanticism as a matter of pure self-preservation. The many compromises effected by the classicists came as a result of dire necessity; those of the romanticists were made, probably, because their authors still remained conscious of their long humanistic inheritance which even the Revolution had not dissipated. And on quite a different level, the middle course of Scribe and his followers rested very simply on their feeling for the immediate demands of the theatrical market.

Les Jeunes France broke no lances over Scribe's theories because he had none, or at least none that were published in the form of a manifesto. Whatever dramaturgical principles he subscribed to must be sought in his works themselves. One need not look for lengthy prefaces, for Scribe was chiefly occupied with getting material on the stage that could be readily acted. He did not worry over such things as Hugo's theory of the sublime and the grotesque,[10] any more than he was concerned with Vigny's ideas about the social mission and duties of the poet.[11] He was obviously less interested in setting forth any ideal program of dramatic art than in demonstrating in a multitude of examples what a stage work in his day should contain to be a popular success.

He stood for the largest body of dramatists in France: the professional writers who turned out material to order. Then, as now, they were responsible for the bulk of the dramatic production of the day. Their number was legion and their names are mostly forgotten except for the master *faiseur*, Scribe, whose technique was a model and whose success was an inspiration for his lesser-known colleagues.

None of them, not even Scribe, took part in the struggle between Romanticism and Classicism. Battles were fought and won, but he remained a neutral, holding his public "as firmly after the success of *Antony* and *Hernani* as before the publication of the preface to *Cromwell*." [12] Disproving the belief that the world was divided into two camps—classic and romantic—these men went their way, impelled by no burning desire to mold the course of dramatic history or to do anything but follow the imperious pattern of popular taste. When the vogue lit on Romanticism they styled their works to fit, and as it shifted so did they. Not in the advance guard nor in the rear echelon, they marched with the crowd, for that was where the rewards were greatest.

Scribe's attachment to the cause of Romanticism was obviously not very intense. That he consorted with it at all, however, was not only significant for French opera but is also a matter of some importance in the history of the romantic movement. It suggests, for instance, that Romanticism, far from being solely the ivory-towered retreat of a few selected votaries, had room for men of many temperaments and degrees of persuasion. By nature, Romanticism was inclusive rather than exclusive. It was not one idea but a whole complex of ideas resting upon the dual assumptions that life is both infinitely varied and grandly unified. The desire in the arts to capture faithfully the color and character of each specific experience or object was complemented by a sense of expansiveness limited only by the size of the world and the capacity of the human mind to comprehend it. With a range of subject matter and treatment so great it is not surprising then to find reflections of Romanticism almost anywhere—even in Scribe. The number of men who contributed distinctively to the romantic culture of ideas is small in comparison with the vastly greater number who took up these views in one form or another and adapted them to their own purposes. Romanticism's real strength, in fact, lay in its possibilities for extension beyond the confines of the *cénacle* which nurtured it originally.

If the movement had been restricted to the handful of literary masters who presented Romanticism in its fullest dress, opera, at least in France, would have been much the poorer; for these men, in the time-honored French literary tradition, were remarkably little concerned with the fate and fortune of the musical theater. The opera libretto was a form almost wholly untouched by the foremost French authors of the period, although the majority of them evinced more than a passing interest in music. Stendhal, who talked and wrote about music and musicians all his life, felt that chance alone prevented him from being a composer. Vigny was strongly attracted to the art—particularly to the great Viennese classical school—and was one of the first to recognize the genius of Berlioz. Balzac frequented the Opéra and wrote two novels that are intimately concerned with music: *Gambara* (1839), containing a spirited analysis of Meyerbeer's *Robert le Diable,* and *Massimilla Doni* (1839), which includes an almost delirious commentary on Rossini's *Moïse.* Madame de Staël, Gérard de Nerval, Lamartine, Musset, and Gautier all had a more or less developed musical taste, while for George Sand the pleasure in music was literally a passion which colored both her life and her books. Perhaps not many of the romanticists were as catholic in taste as Emile Deschamps, who "liked equally the music of Meyerbeer and Cimarosa, Schubert and Donizetti, Rossini and Berlioz," but of the important French romantic authors only Chateaubriand and Mérimée seem to have been comparatively limited in their response to music.[13] As far as opera was concerned, however, all this affection was love at a distance, in spite of the fact that *musique* was synonymous in the Frenchman's vocabulary with the lyric stage.[14]

There was a great deal of talk about the ideal synthesis of the arts, but most of the eminent literary figures balked when it came to the point of walking to the altar to consummate the union. Some exceptions may be observed but they are not numerous. Gautier wrote the scenarios to several ballets, of which *Giselle* (1841, music by Adolphe Adam) is the most famous. Vigny read the book written by Auguste Barbier and Leon Wailly for Berlioz's *Benvenuto Cellini* (1835–1837) and gave his advice to its authors; and Hugo, yielding to the pressure put on him to make a libretto from his book, *Notre Dame de Paris,* turned out for Louise Bertin the failure entitled *L'Esmerelda* (1836). For the most part, though, as in the eighteenth century, the French poets and dramatists held aloof from any working agreements with musicians. Since their betters would have none of it, the rapprochement between the arts was thus left, as R. L. Evans observed, to secondary poets like Deschamps, Barbier, and Wailly.[15] But above all it rested in the hands of the most unpoetic of playwrights: Scribe.

In one sense, therefore, Scribe gained his preeminent position in French opera by default. It appears that those who might conceivably have challenged him were too little interested in the matter to spend any effort on it. Indifference, however, is probably not the whole of the answer. A fuller explanation may well include the assumption that the romantic poets instinctively shied away from a labor which would inevitably curb the exercise of their lyric powers. Words flowed freely after their long imprisonment behind the stilted, authoritarian barriers of pseudo-classicism, and poets were loath to impose any new hindrances to their movement. Since some restriction is a condition of union, poetry preferred to remain in its solitary state.

From this, one is led to the conclusion that Romanticism in literature, as far as it meant a revolution of language, a renovation of the word to make it more supple, colorful, and sonorous, was by nature somewhat inimical to the requirements of the opera libretto. Certainly the change in vocabulary, bringing the substitution of the *mot propre* for the elevated paraphrase of Classicism, was not in itself a source of alarm. Danger only arose when language was given free rein to flower into the full lyricism so characteristic of romantic poetry. For different reasons, both the libretto and the spoken drama had cause to be wary of that development.

It is significant that the lyrical quality of the romantic drama rests in inverse ratio to its fortune in the theater. Alexandre Dumas, in many ways the most influential romantic dramatist in France, was also one of the writers least concerned with literary niceties or high poetical beauty. Where he succeeded, Victor Hugo failed. The latter's plays, with all their magnificent verse, came to an unhappy end with *Les Burgraves* (1843). Fascinated by the sound of his character's voices, he allowed his ambitious attempt to bring poetry to the stage to be drowned in its own rhetorical splendor.

If the playwright, from the experience of Hugo, has to acknowledge that "pathos and lyric sonority, in however ample measure, are not materials out of which alone a dramatic edifice can be constructed," [16] so the librettist perforce must reconcile his joy in the play of words to the inexorable needs of the composer. He must realize that any prolixity in the book is multiplied several times in the music. There is no single *right* kind of libretto, but the principle is common to all opera that the poet should be discreet in his flights of lyricism in order to allow music sufficient field for expression. Opera, whatever its style may be, is incapable of absorbing too rich a mixture of poetry. Pietro Metastasio (1698–1782), the eighteenth century's greatest librettist, whose mobile, elegant verse flooded the Italian lyric theater, never forgot that axiom. Even the classic French opera of Lully, though firmly governed by the text, is not overladen with a wealth of verbal attractions. Lully insured that when he chose as his librettist the talented but limited Quinault. He realized that if music is to conserve its own kind of lyric beauty and maintain its own essential prerogatives, its composer of necessity must insist on a librettist who displays the modesty becoming to a partner in a corporate work such as opera.

Modesty, however, was not a common virtue among romantic authors. The wonderful liberation of language, which put such abundant life again into poetry, so intoxicated the poets that acceptance of the terms of opera composition became impossible for them. It was necessary for musicians to go elsewhere for their librettos, and the road to Scribe was open. The latter had already proved himself in *opéra-comique* and was in high favor with the theater public. A craftsman at heart and a collaborator by trade, he could enter into an alliance with music unhampered either by fears or by reservations.

Composers, too, could work with him without endangering any of their jealously-guarded rights. Scribe knew his role and held himself to it, displaying the rare ability in his relations with musicians to strike a happy mean between subservience and dictation. He neither effaced himself too completely before the composer, nor on the other hand, did he try to write librettos which were actually independent plays complete in themselves without benefit of music. He appreciated that "each art in its own domain has the right to be lord and master," [17] and was willing to give music its head at any suitable moment. But he also knew his countrymen well enough to realize, in the words of another contemporary journal, that there was a large French public which would "never be captivated sufficiently by the charm of music to overlook defects in the libretto." [18]

Bearing that in mind, Scribe constructed his opera books as carefully as his comedies. As he went from the intimate stage of *vaudeville* to the more spacious frame of grand opera he naturally worked with broader strokes, yet the move brought no visible relaxation in his standards of design. Whatever faults there may be, they are not errors of composition. Scribe brought no poetry to the Opéra, but he did come equipped with an unexcelled skill in play-making and with a clear knowledge of his duties and responsibilities as a librettist. One may question Véron when he said that Scribe was, "of all dramatic authors, the one who best understood opera." [19] Nevertheless, it must be admitted in the light of the aims and the resources of French grand opera that Scribe did "excel in the choice of subjects, . . . in creating interesting musical situations to fit the genius of the composer; and his scripts always provided favorable opportunities for the varied and original effects of the *mise en scène* which were rightly demanded of a director." [20] Under his guidance the opera learned the secrets of the popular theater, and the well-made libretto took its place alongside the well-made play.

VII

THE LIBRETTO

S CRIBE'S WIDE experience in the popular theater and in *opéra-comique* had trained him in his craft and had sharpened his judgment of public sentiment to such an extent that no preliminary fumbling was necessary when he applied himself to serious opera. From the start, his work in the latter genre was firm and settled in its outlines. It was an achievement whose importance becomes readily apparent if one glances at the history of the French opera libretto from 1671 to 1831. A bird's-eye view of that era reveals two distinct periods of stability: one at the beginning and another at the end of the long span. The first was dominated by Philippe Quinault (1635–1688), the second by Scribe. Each of these writers enjoyed a monopoly powerful enough to subdue competition in his day and to establish a style of libretto whose influence on the lyric stage was decisive and far-reaching. Between them lay the whole of the eighteenth century—a time filled with a multitude of new hopes, trends, and accomplishments, but as far as opera in France was concerned, a time also that clung to remnants of the past as it advanced hesitantly into the future. There were many indications of the changes to come, yet no clear line was fixed in either the sung or the spoken drama until after the Revolution dealt its fatal blow to the authority of tradition. The long step from Quinault to Scribe could then be completed.

SUBJECT MATTER

It was a step that stretched from abstraction to actuality, from court opera to opera designed especially for the bourgeoisie. As the audience changed, so did the subject matter of the libretto. In the seventeenth century when opera was in part a glorification of the monarch, it was held that only mythological subjects were suitable to the lyric stage and that gods, demi-gods, and royal persons were essential characters in the plot because they assured the necessary elevation and grandeur to the entertainment. In that respect lyric drama resembled the spoken tragedy of the time; but there the similarity ended. The regularity of structure and the intellectual tone of a play by Racine are as foreign to Quinault's librettos as they are to the works of Alexandre Hardy. To be sure, French opera in the *Grand Siècle* was called *tragédie-lyrique* and one finds critics who upheld the libretto as a true literary genre in its own right, worthy of comparison to the best examples of spoken drama. "There are few tragedies or comedies finer than the majority of Quinault's works," said one author.[1] Yet, as René Guiet pointed out in his excellent study, *L'Evolution d'un genre: le livret d'opéra en France de Gluck à la Révolution,* most writers of the time were more concerned with the differences than with the resemblances between opera and classical tragedy. "Tragédie-lyrique" is an expression that "has only the value of a general term and seems to signify merely the serious theater set to music."[2] The essential distinction between spoken and lyric tragedy was brought out by Charles Batteux when he said that the one was "heroic" and was called simply "tragedy," while the other was "marvelous" and was named "lyric spectacle or opera."[3]

There is no doubt that the employment of the marvelous or the supernatural was a vital feature of the classical French opera, whose purpose was to "surprise, amuse, and lead one from illusion to illusion."[4] That characteristic more than anything else pinned lyric drama to fabulous subjects. Since the supernatural had no relation to the probabilities of actual life, the French opera borrowed its subject matter almost exclusively from Greek and Roman mythology or from the more recent fables of Ariosto and Tasso. In that world of miracles there was room for the things that delighted the frequenters of the Académie Royale de Musique: for the delicate gallantry of Quinault's language, the multiplication of amorous intrigue, the constant reliance upon divine intervention in the plot, and the use of the complicated machinery that was introduced into France from the Italian stage.

As long as Lully retained his prestige there was little change in that pattern. From the time of Saint-Evremond (1613–1703) French authors criticized the opera for its excesses; but it was not until the middle of the eighteenth century that objection linked with boredom became strong enough to make a breach in the established order. In this matter France was at least fifty years behind Italy. The latter country had already gone through a period of reaction against the older opera of mythology and out of it came the "reform" librettos of Apostolo Zeno (1668–1750), the scholar and playwright who preceded Metastasio as the Imperial Court Poet in Vienna. Turning to historical subjects in the laudable attempt to prune from the libretto some of its former irregularities and give it greater dramatic truth, he opened the way for the smoother, more elegant and better known works of his younger contemporary. Both men were highly esteemed in France and Metastasio, called *Il Sofocle Italiano* in his day, enjoyed a world-wide reputation as a dramatist of the first rank.

These Italian librettos were supplemented by the lively critical work of Francesco Algarotti (1712–1764) entitled *Saggio sopra l'Opera in Musica* (1750), which was evidently well known to the French advocates of reform. Algarotti's appeal for a tighter dramatic structure was echoed by the leading literary men in France, who found themselves quite unable to abandon reason to the marvels of fantasy. Rousseau urged that the miraculous was as well placed in the epic poem as it was ridiculous in the theater.[5] "Deliver me from the puerile genre you call marvelous," said Baron Grimm, "because it is marvelous only for you and for children." [6] In Diderot's opinion also "the world of magic can amuse infants," but "reason is pleased only by the real world." [7]

Dispute over the representation of the supernatural in opera reached its climax in the so-called "buffoon quarrel" precipitated by the performance in Paris in 1752 of Pergolesi's *La Serva Padrona*.

This simple, human story served as a rallying point for the philosophers who demanded the employment of less imaginary subject matter. History was the obvious source of the newly-sought verisimilitude, and following the path taken by Voltaire in *Zaïre* (1732) and *Tancrède* (1760) and by De Belloy in *Le Siège de Calais* (1765), there appeared a few operas which turned away from mythology. They were not numerous, but mention may be made of *Ernelinde* (1767) by Poinsinet and Philidor, *Adèle de Ponthieu* (1772) by Razius de St. Marc and La Borde, and *Sabinus* (1774) by Chabanon and Gossec. The first was concerned with the history of Norway, the second with that of France, and the last dealt with an episode in the history of Gaul.[8]

It would be idle to pretend, however, that the influence of Quinault was dead. The same years that produced the three historical operas mentioned above also brought forth works in the old tradition such as *Thésée* (1767) by Quinault and Mondonville, *Amadis de Gaule* (1771) by Quinault and La Borde, and *L'Union de l'Amour et des Arts* (1773) by Le Monnier and Floquet. There were still people who agreed with Charles Perrault that nothing can be too fabulous for an opera book, and that the ancient tales "make the finest subjects and give greater pleasure than better conducted and more regular plots." [9] Some said that music and the supernatural went hand in hand, that the fictions of mythology made the conventions of a sung language more acceptable.[10] Others argued that the marvelous had a happy influence on the variety of the *mise en scène,* and that it was always necessary for the sake of the décors to choose subjects from mythology or from fairy tales.[11] "The prodigies, the variety, and the spectacular pomp that must accompany the grand opera, oblige authors to take nearly all their subjects from the world of fable. The adventures of the gods of mythology and the marvels that they are supposed to perform furnish incidents which are quite in accord with the nature of the lyric spectacle. By comparison, history opens only a sterile field to the theater." [12] Nevertheless, the movement for change in the French lyric drama was gaining headway. Spurred on by the philosophers and by the Italian examples in theory and practice, the opera began to lop off many of its excesses even before Gluck appeared.

The production then in 1774 of *Iphigénie en Aulide*, Gluck's first original French opera, was favored by a certain amount of precedent, although it undoubtedly represents a definite stage in the history of the French libretto. It was a phase marked by a return of the librettist, Bailli du Roullet (1716–1786), to the model of Racine in an attempt to clear away the superfluities and irregularities of character and plot that had separated opera from the classical French drama. *Iphigénie en Aulide* and its two successors—*Orphée et Euridice,* given in Paris in 1774, and *Alceste,* presented there in 1776—demonstrated clearly the ideas of French reform circles in regard to the necessity for greater simplicity and unity of construction. However, none of these operas cut wholly away from the ties of the older style. Each used the subject matter of the ancient legend and all retained the happy ending and the *deus ex machina* so characteristic of the earlier period.

This juxtaposition of the old and the new was distinctive of the closing years in the eighteenth century. Traditionalists continued to advance the merits of Quinault, and musicians still used his poems. *Armide* was set by Gluck himself in 1777, and three more of Quinault's librettos soon reappeared in the adaptations of Marmontel: *Roland* (1778) and *Atys* (1780) with music by Piccini, and *Persée* (1780) in a setting by Philidor. At the same time *Le Seigneur Bienfaisant* (1780) by Rochon de Chabannes and Floquet daringly presented a bourgeois subject at the Académie. Other operas like *Louis IX en Egypte* (1790) by Guillard and Le Moyne with its setting laid in medieval France, and *Arvire et Evelina* (1788) by Guillard and Sacchini which went farther back to Celtic times, tried to avoid routine by dipping into past history for their materials. One sees a variety of trends, but there was no longer a single ruling type of libretto.

Opera, like drama, was a house divided against itself. The one playwright in France at the time who realized completely the problems of the lyric stage was Beaumarchais whose preface to *Tarare* (1787) is a masterly and thoroughly modern essay on operatic dramaturgy and esthetics. Rejecting both mythology and history as sources of subject matter, he proposed that opera should sweep away the boundaries of tragedy and comedy and incorporate all genres into one inclusive form. His plea for a style of drama that would embrace the full complexity of human life was a direct anticipation of romantic theory, but it had relatively little effect upon the immediate course of French opera. The lyric drama continued to follow its uncertain path of the last few years. Quinault's dynasty had fallen, but no other had been established in its place and none was installed until the advent of Scribe.

In the years remaining before his appearance, many kinds of librettos found their way to the stage of the Académie. Some were new while others merely followed eighteenth-century lines of construction. Opera, however, as well as music in general, was becoming more and more sensitive to the movement of literary and philosophical ideas and to the pressure of political events. Out of the Revolution came the so-called "horror" operas such as Cherubini's *Lodoiska* (1791) and Le Sueur's *La Caverne* (1793). Frankly topical works were also produced in abundance. *L'Offrande à la Liberté* (1792) by Gardel and Gossec, which was written expressly to bring in the words "allons, enfants de la patrie," was one of the most popular in a series that included *Le Triomphe de la République* (1793) by M. J. Chénier and Gossec, *Le Siège de Thionville* (1793) by Saulnier and Jadin, and *La Réunion du 10 Août* (1794) by Moline and Porta. These productions "of, by, and for the people" were supplemented by other pieces such as *Miltiade à Marathon* (1793) by Guillard and Le Moyne, and *Horatius Coclès* (1794) by Arnault and Méhul, which were also in a heroic vein although inspired by ancient history. At this time the Opéra "was without doubt the theater that contributed above all others to inflame the public spirit with its patriotic scenes." [13] As it had glorified the *Roi Soleil* in the *Ancien Régime,* the lyric stage now honored the struggles of the people.

With the passing of the revolutionary period the Opéra returned to a quieter existence. In a few instances it showed some relation to more modern thought, but the reestablishment of the older repertory brought back the indecisiveness that characterized the latter part of the eighteenth century. The Ossianic legend, which interested Chateaubriand so greatly, reached the Opéra in Le Sueur's *Ossian ou les Bardes* (1804). The exotic story found expression in Dalayrac's *Le Pavillon du Calife* (1804), and more recent historical subjects were used in Spontini's *Fernand Cortez* (1809) and in *Roger de Sicile* (1817) by Guy and Berton. The revival of religious feeling that followed after the trials of the Revolution and that was furthered by Napoleon with the Concordat of September, 1801, brought forth a mild wave of operas on Biblical subjects early in the nineteenth century, among which may be mentioned *La Mort d'Adam et son Apothéose* (1809) by Guillard and Le Sueur and Kreutzer's *Abel* (1810). Finally, it should be observed that some librettos still depended on the repertory of the Comédie-Française for material. *Sémiramis*, put to music by Catel in 1802, and *Olympie*, composed by Spontini in 1819, were adaptations of tragedies by Voltaire; Rudolph Kreutzer's *Aristippe* (1808) was an imitation of Andrieux's play *Anaximandre;* and Spontini's *La Vestale* (1807) and *Fernand Cortez* (1809), the two great successes of the Restoration, were both adapted from earlier plays by Fontenelle and Piron respectively.[14]

It is difficult to believe that the Opéra in company with the Théâtre-Français should have halted on the outskirts of Romanticism until almost the third decade of the nineteenth century, yet such was the case. Before then the weakening forces of Classicism still contested the right of the official stages to enter the newer world of ideas. In 1827, the year that produced the preface to *Cromwell,* a critic of the lyric theater felt it necessary once more to raise his voice against the bedraggled remnants of the *tragédie-lyrique.* "I think it is time," he said, "to relegate to the storehouse all the Greek, Roman and mythological frippery. Homer and Virgil have been honored long enough at the Opéra. We must look for another species of wonderment, perhaps less classic, but more pleasing and in keeping with the demands of our new literature." There was an inexhaustible source of subject matter, he added, in the old French chronicles and fables, and in the popular traditions and beliefs of the Middle Ages. "Rich in originality and in imagination, they offer all the elements required for the success of an opera. The only lack is a skillful man to put them to use." [15]

The Académie had waited a long time for that "skillful man," but these words of J. T. Merle were hardly in print before he appeared. With the engagement of Scribe to write for the Opéra in 1828 the years of uncertainty for the French libretto came to an end. Henceforth the destinies of the opera book rested in the hands of this one playwright. As Quinault was to Lully, so was Scribe to the composers in Véron's organization, for during the latter's management not one new opera was produced which did not bear the label "book by Scribe." At the Académie Royale de Musique he came to hold as great a monopoly as he enjoyed at the Théâtre du Gymnase. He had already guided the popular *vaudeville* into new channels and had put his stamp on the *opéra-comique;* now he was to determine the form and style of the distinctive opera libretto of the 1830's.

Between 1828 and 1836 nine operas with librettos by Scribe were produced at the Académie. Four of these, however, do not belong to the pattern of grand opera and need not detain us. *Le Comte Ory* (1828) was a revision of a *comédie mêlée de chansons* which had been popular in 1816 at the Théâtre du Vaudeville; *Le Philtre* (1831) was a brilliantly successful farce; *Le Serment ou les Faux Monnayeurs* (1832) was another bit of frivolity that received a much cooler welcome than its predecessors; and *Ali-Baba ou les Quarante Voleurs* (1833) was a four-act tale from the Arabian nights linked to the current style in serious opera more by its colorful scenery than by anything else. The five remaining works: *La Muette de Portici* (1828), *Robert le Diable* (1831), *Gustave III* (1833), *La Juive* (1835), and *Les Huguenots* (1836), with the addition of Rossini's *Guillaume Tell* (1829), changed the whole course of French lyric drama and formed the keystones of the grand opera structure.

The revolution Scribe effected was complete. Casting aside the faded materials of lyric tragedy, he also avoided any adaptation of established works from the spoken stage. Apart from *Guillaume Tell* (1829), with which Scribe was not concerned, no libretto in the line of grand opera was a made-over play, even though the actual subjects in a few cases had been used before. The Naples Revolution of 1647, for instance, was presented both in *La Muette de Portici* and in the drama, *Masaniello,* by Moreau and Lafortelle; while *Les Huguenots* was based on the same historical event that is found in Chénier's *Charles IX* and in Mérimée's *Chronique du temps de Charles IX*. There was no question in these librettos, however, of remodelling familiar pieces.

Scribe's position in this matter was fully seconded by the composer Meyerbeer, who had quite definite opinions against such adaptations. The ancient tragedies, he felt, were too far removed in spirit from the music of his day to be useful, and he believed that later masterpieces such as *Hamlet, Faust, Le Cid,* or *Le Misanthrope* were unsuitable for musical setting because they lead a life of their own, complete in themselves without need of any outside assistance. "One does not redo what has already been done perfectly." [16]

Scribe, then, with the endorsement of Meyerbeer, sought his subjects in commoner ground. Ever alert to the state of the public mind, he wrote as people thought and chose his materials from the stream of popular opinion. Véron related that Scribe, whether engaged in business or in pleasure, constantly made note of characters or situations that might be dramatized. "He observed and listened more than he spoke." [17] If it is true that Hugo only seized and condensed ideas already in the air,[18] it is even surer that Scribe was a sounding board for the vibrations of public taste. Letting others of a more combative nature write the pamphlets and prefaces, he was content to follow along, making capital of any prevailing ideas and predilections he found useful.

He took advantage, for example, of the vogue for Gothic romances that swept France shortly before he began writing for the Opéra. These were imaginative stories of the supernatural, filled with mysterious and frightful beings who moved in a gloomy atmosphere through the subterranean chambers and secret passageways of medieval castles and monasteries. Given its earliest effective expression in Horace Walpole's *Castle of Otranto* (1764), the tale of fantasy and terror was immensely popular in England during the late eighteenth century. From there it migrated to France in company with Bürger's *Lenore* (1773), Goethe's *Sorcerer's Apprentice* (1797), and a quantity of similar ballads of the supernatural or the macabre; but the full effect of this type of literature on French writers was not felt until the third decade of the nineteenth century when the tales of E. T. A. Hoffmann were imported from Germany.

Interest then in the fantastic reached a climax in France which was reflected at the Opéra in 1831 with the production of *Robert le Diable*.

This work has for its subject an old theme: the contest for a man's soul between Good and Evil. Robert is a young knight who has had the misfortune to be born of a woman wedded to a devil. His own nature at first inclines towards that of his father, and his misdeeds are so numerous that he, too, is thought to be in league with the Evil One. In due time, however, he meets a lady named Isabelle whose love he seeks and whose purity causes him to reconsider his mode of life. Thereafter he is subjected to the conflicting pressures of his mother and Isabelle on the one hand, and of Bertram, his father in disguise, on the other. Bertram has been permitted to leave Hell by his superiors in order to win Robert for their service, and through the use of various supernatural devices he appears to be on the road to success. At the last minute, though, before his term on earth expires, the tide is turned against him by a belated appeal that Robert receives from his mother. Bertram is then swallowed up in flames and Robert is saved for his beautiful bride.

Latter-day audiences of course are quite accustomed to seeing their operatic heroes lured from the path of virtue by the supernatural seducer appearing in one form or another. Witness Tannhauser's adventures with Venus, Faust's compact with Mephistopheles, or more lately, Jabez Stone's negotiations with Scratch in *The Devil and Daniel Webster*. All of these actions reached the lyric stage since the date of *Robert le Diable;* but it had its predecessors, too, notably *Der Freischütz*, in which Max succumbs to the wiles of Caspar for the sake of obtaining the magic bullets.

The story of *Robert* was inspired by an old legend which evidently had existed at an earlier period in the form of a mystery play; but the libretto by all reports has little in common with its source. Adolphe Jullien, who looked into the matter, said "there is only one real point of contact between the mystery and the opera: the birth of Robert conceived as a work of the Devil." Apparently the title figure itself underwent the greatest change in transmission. Scribe, "wishing to present his hero sympathetically," softened his character considerably by omitting from his career "those monstrous crimes, those odious atrocities, which the legend so generously attributed to him." [19] Nevertheless, the librettist managed to concoct a romanesque tale that was probably no less or no more "medieval" than most stories of its kind, and that gave ample play to the fantastic legendary elements of superstition which fascinated the opera public of 1830. In making use of a medieval legend, Scribe of course was neither breaking new ground nor was he exemplifying a platform. *Der Freischütz*, which was "arranged" and presented to Paris in 1824 as *Robin des Bois,* had already shown the way, and Scribe was much too busy a man to sit down in the manner of Richard Wagner and elaborate a theory in favor of librettos based on legends dealing with the supernatural. It was sufficient that Weber's opera had been a success and that the public was interested in things medieval.

People at the time delighted especially in the imagined picturesqueness of the Middle Ages; but in a broader sense they also had become more conscious of history, of the past of France and its neighbors. The Revolution and the marches of Napoleon had given men a new feeling for the movement of events. Their eyes were opened and their minds were unlocked to the images of faraway places. "They dreamed of the snows of Moscow and of the sun on the Pyramids," said Alfred De Musset.[20] Those who grew up in the early 1800's rediscovered their source in the history of their country, for they saw in it "the grandiose extension of their own obscure personalities through the centuries." [21]

This attitude was reflected everywhere in the world of literature and the theater as well as in the field of scholarship. The tenuous romance breathed nostalgically of the past, while national history and common tradition furnished plots for countless plays in the secondary theaters of Paris. The historical melodrama, in fact, was by far the most popular form of production on the Boulevard.[22] Historical novels, too, were written in quantity, and the stories of Walter Scott in particular, which appeared in France for the first time in 1816, enjoyed a tremendous circulation.[23] Archeologists labored to restore the monuments of medieval times and historians added their learning to the more idealized creations of the novelists.

Bolstered by the brilliant school of historical writing which came into being with the work of Fauriel, Thierry, Barante, Guizot, and Michelet, the recreation of characters, events, and settings from the past was increasingly favored in the major theaters of Paris. Writers like Mme. de Staël and Stendhal gave their support to "grand national subjects" for the drama; [24] while from abroad came Goethe's *Goetz von Berlichingen* (1773), the plays of Schiller, and especially the works of Shakespeare to serve as models of what might be accomplished by a dramatist with the great moments in a nation's history.

For many years there had been intermittent presentations at the Académie of historical scenes and characters, but by the time of Scribe public opinion had solidified enough to make the practice general. None of the important grand operas produced in Paris from *La Muette* to *Les Huguenots* failed to respond to that mandate. *La Muette de Portici* dramatized the short, colorful career of Masaniello, the fisherman who led the revolt of the Neapolitans against their Spanish overlords in 1647. *Guillaume Tell* made use of a stirring period in Swiss history when the cantons struck at their Austrian masters. *Gustave III* brought to the stage the figure of that art-loving monarch of Sweden. The Council of Constance formed the background of *La Juive;* and *Les Huguenots* dealt with the fierce religious strife which agitated France in the sixteenth century.

In all these works, however, the historical material in itself merely provided an occasion or a setting for the action devised by the librettist. While writers like Ludovic Vitet and Prosper Mérimée made serious though publicly unrewarded attempts to create realistic plays which adhered closely to recorded facts, Scribe, as Taine said of Walter Scott, stopped "in the vestibule of history." [25] One looks vainly in grand opera for a faithful union of historical method and dramatic technique, for the librettist made no pretense of being a scholar. Scribe was neither embarrassed with history nor with theories about it. He simply employed the existing knowledge of the past as it suited him without being disturbed if reality were disfigured in the process. In *La Muette,* for instance, he utilized the historical fact that there was such a man as Masianello who led the popular forces of Naples in revolution, but embellished it with the legend concerning his poisoning by a beverage which is supposed to have affected his reason. Furthermore, both history and legend were supplemented by a tale of pure imagination: the tragic story of Masaniello's sister Fenella, a mute who was deceived and deserted by Alfonso, son of the Spanish Viceroy. Fiction and fact were joined in the one work, but it is obvious that the former occupied the larger place. In *La Muette*, as in all of his grand operas, Scribe used history mostly as a background or a scaffolding upon which to build a series of stirring incidents of his own invention.

Although the amount of actual history one sees in grand opera is small, it is about the same as he finds in melodrama or in the romantic drama of the time. Pixérécourt was fond of historical subjects, but in the popular theater for which he wrote "the adjective *'historique'* soon acquired so broad a meaning that it was applied to drama based on possibility or probability." [26] Likewise, on France's premier stage the conception of a national, historical tragedy, which had tempted playwrights for a hundred years, became greatly diluted after the production of *Henri III et sa cour* in 1829. That play was a genuine success, yet its creator, Alexandre Dumas, "never again risked getting so close to history." [27] Dramatists like Pixérécourt, Scribe and Dumas saw what a resource they had in the picturesque scenery of former days; and at the same time they also realized that the scholar's view of history was apt to be too precise and inflexible for popular dramatic treatment.

On the Boulevard, at the Opéra, and at the Théâtre-Français authors thus went to the past for its color and its names, but they looked to the present for the substance of their works. They took their themes and drew their inspiration from the doctrines and actualities of the contemporary world which was more and more occupied after the July Revolution with a multitude of social and economic problems. "Poetry will no longer be lyric, . . . epic . . . dramatic," said Lamartine. "It will be philosophical, religious, political, or social, corresponding to the periods traversed by mankind." [28] A large part of society was in a questioning mood, and the spirit was magnified among the Romanticists. Instead of retiring from the scene they pushed forward. By 1830 the artistic and literary battles were won, but the fight for social reform had only begun. Following its earlier, more individualistic phase, Romanticism now trained its sights to include the welfare of the whole people. The poor, the unfortunate, the dispossessed—all the victims of an imperfect social order—poured out their plaints through the pens of the romantic authors. Poets, dramatists, and novelists took their places with the philosophers and economists in the great task of advancing liberal ideas of social justice and of political and religious equality.

In the forefront of this activity was the Théâtre-Français, and following at a modest distance came the Opéra. Unsupported by theory and neglected by the avowed Romanticists, the lyric theater nevertheless was clearly marked by the liberal program of thought. The librettos were set in earlier periods of history, but they achieved timeliness by indirection, since their themes were such that they might easily be related to controversies of the day. *La Muette* and *Guillaume Tell* pictured the struggle of oppressed peoples against political tyranny. *La Juive* portrayed the harsh fate of a Jewish minority living in the midst of a hostile Christian population; and *Les Huguenots* continued the tragic story of religious intolerance as it pitted Catholics against Protestants in the bloody strife climaxed by the massacre of Saint Bartholomew's Night. All of these works were concerned with freedom of one kind or another. By this much, at least, French opera escaped from the morass of a worn-out mythology into the more invigorating atmosphere of a Romanticism actively engaged in exposing the defects and presenting plans for the betterment of society.

Scribe thus brought the Opéra to earth and furnished it with subject matter which was in tune with contemporary life and interests. He never forgot, however, that he was primarily a business man, not a social philosopher. Though his subjects were liberal in tone, they were always surrounded by a sufficient amount of common moralizing to make them wholly acceptable to the bourgeois audience for which he wrote. He was alert enough to stay abreast of his day and shrewd enough to realize that Romanticism penetrated everywhere to some degree; yet, whether working in opera or in *vaudeville*, he was at all times the popular dramatist, holding himself to what he thought the traffic would bear. He neither ran ahead of his field nor lagged behind it, for in whatever he did "Scribe had the merit of writing for the public, not against it." [29]

CHARACTERS AND ACTION

Since the themes of grand opera were broadly concerned with questions of freedom and oppression, it is to be expected that the characters in these dramas should be drawn from more than one rank of society. Commoners and nobles were both introduced, and most frequently were set off one against the other. In *La Muette* we are shown the humble Fenella and the princely Alfonso; in *Guillaume Tell* we meet Tell the peasant and Gesler the arrogant officer of the Crown; and in *La Juive* the unfortunate Jews, Rachel and Eléazar, are linked with the noble Leopold and with Brogni, a Cardinal of the Church. *Les Huguenots* also presents the contrast between Raoul, an obscure Huguenot knight, and the powerful Catholic Court. Among the characters of lower estate, Tell alone emerges victorious and unscathed from the conflict with power and authority. For the rest, persons of common birth or weaker position customarily suffer in one way or another at the hands of those in higher stations of life.

Scribe, like Hugo who often tried to show the lords of the earth in the worst possible light, was patently for the victims against their oppressors. The comparison in grand opera between persons of high and low degree always favors the latter, and in most cases small effort was made to mitigate the offenses of the clergy and nobles. Gesler is an out-and-out scoundrel; Saint-Bris and his Catholic followers are militant religious fanatics; while Brogni, though showing some signs of compassion, still feels impelled by his office and his faith to carry out their bloody orders against the non-conforming Huguenots.

The noblemen, Alfonso and Leopold, fare badly too, although they appear less vicious than weak. Their weakness is strikingly shown in contrast to the strength of the women betrayed by them. Each of the two men disguises his rank and steps out of his class to make love to a woman far below him in the social scale. Alfonso deceives Fenella, a poor mute, and Leopold misleads the young Jewess Rachel. The noblemen regret their amorous digressions, but are quite willing to drop them when they appear to be getting out of hand. Opposing this easy solution, however, are two strong-willed women of the lower classes who resent being thrown aside.

Here, as in most grand operas of the time, love is treated from a feminine point of view. The men concerned are notoriously unstable in their emotions. Either they wander astray from their actual or intended wives, or they indulge in such outrageous exhibitions of childish temper and jealousy as to make the lives of their companions a nightmare. Gustave, although infatuated with another man's wife, is the only male lover who comports himself with any degree of dignity. The women, on the other hand, are steadfast, understanding, self-sacrificing and forgiving. Not all of them are notable additions to operatic literature, but each shows to some extent the virtues of the stronger members of the sex, and for the most part they are distinctly more admirable individuals than the men they love. Alfonso and Leopold are weaklings who have defied the laws of society but shrink when faced with retribution, while Raoul is of that violent, impatient, and immature race whose prototype in the French romantic drama is the Antony of Alexandre Dumas. The women alone show any real constancy and nobility in their emotions. Each is treated badly by her lover, but after an inward struggle all end by being generous even to death.

The romantic woman of passion and conviction was a vastly different creature from her classical predecessor who had existed largely as an object of a polite and sensuous gallantry. She could no longer be treated merely as "man's toy, an agreeable partner in pleasure who helps him while away the tedium of the hours." [80] Rousseau had opened a new life to her as man's equal, and the nineteenth century saw that promise begin to unfold. Some writers like Chateaubriand and Lamartine idealized her; others thought of her more as a person of flesh and blood and concerned themselves with the social problems arising out of the higher regard in which she was held. While melodrama viewed with righteous horror any portrayal of physical passion, it was an essential part of romantic drama, linked with the new conceptions of the social character of love and its rights or penalties when it runs counter to the conventions and laws of society.

Grand opera, too, recognized and made capital of the tremendous force of passionate love. Scribe understood the unique power of music to heighten its expression and his librettos always afforded the composer opportunities in that direction. Yet only in *Robert le Diable* and *Gustave III* does the drama of human love appear to be presented for its own sake. In *La Juive,* for instance, it can never be dissociated from the main theme of religious prejudice that dominates the work. Without this, Leopold's affair with Rachel becomes a mere princely peccadillo which may be reprehensible enough but hardly calls for state vengeance on the innocent girl. Here as elsewhere in grand opera the emotion of love gained dramatic importance as it was used to light up the major social issues treated by Scribe.

By virtue of these underlying motifs the characters were emphasized less as unique personalities than as social beings representative of large classes or other groups. Subsequent discussion of grand opera music will make this point clearer, but even in the librettos alone it is evident. Unlike René, who "bore little resemblance to other men," the characters of Scribe generally do not appear conscious of any personal singularity or superiority. They do not feel the awful isolation of Byron's Manfred, nor are they weighed down by the weariness and melancholy of Sénancour's Obermann. To be sure, the librettos contain numerous lines such as these:

> Quel sombre ennui l'accable! [31]
>
> Une vague mélancolie
> Des tourments cruels et secrets
> Consument lentement ma vie
> Qui me fatigue et que je hais! [32]

But reflection on the total expression of the characters indicates that these picturesque phrases are in reality nothing more than window dressing. They are part of that apparatus of dark mystery and foreboding which opera in France inherited from the Gothic tale, rather than an outpouring of the disenchantment felt by a René or a Werther.

Only in *Robert le Diable* do we meet individuals who exist out-side of society or in defiance of it, and even their rebellion is greatly diluted by the conventional poses they assume. Bertram, for all his perverted sense of fatherhood, emerges essentially as just another operatic devil; while in Robert we are confronted merely by rather an unpleasant combination of sentimentality and bravado. The latter indulges in an extraordinary amount of bluster, yet despite his legendary title he never convinces us that he is really a bad man or a strong one. Jullien is quite correct in saying that "what is least diabolical in *Robert le Diable* is Robert himself." [33] In fact, he is fundamentally so characterless that it is a matter of wonder why either Heaven or Hell should be inclined to worry over his destiny. At first glance he might appear to bear some relation to Da Ponte's great figure, Don Giovanni, but the similarity is wholly superficial. Robert is a man who seems to care nothing for the social or moral law and who has a past full of unmentionable crimes. Yet his ef-frontery is sadly lacking in conviction. The Don is grown up, ma-ture in his unredeemability; Robert is merely an errant schoolboy full of a callow cynicism which is dissipated by a milkmaid's appeal to his feelings of filial veneration.

The kind of character represented by Don Giovanni, supremely confident of his powers and defiant of either earthly or supernatural forces, had quite gone out of style at the Opéra. Homely, middle-class virtue held the field. Indeed, it could scarcely be otherwise in a libretto written by Scribe. Like a majority of his class he was a con-servative liberal imbued with the bourgeois respect for legality. In his plays he constantly sustained the sanctity of marriage and the solid virtues of domestic life; and at the Opéra likewise he preserved a strict regard for the tenets of the bourgeois creed. There is no sug-gestion of the individualistic hero wronged by society, nor is there any tendency to glorify revolt against the moral law. Every such lapse ends unhappily. We find that even the servants have ceased the earlier practice of cheating their masters at every opportunity. In-stead, in the persons of Alice and Marcel they act as moral props to their employers. Released, however, from the kind of ending re-quired in *vaudeville* and comedy, Scribe in his operas did not show the possession of virtue to be a guarantee of earthly happiness. On the contrary, in most cases the reward is quite clearly saved for another world. Whatever the results, though, the typical attitude of the Scribian hero or heroine is that of Guillaume Tell who points toward Heaven saying, "Les périls sont bien grands, mais le pilote est là." [34]

That thought is as conventional as the speech is artificial, and both are characteristic of grand opera. For all the interest of the Académie in realistic settings, the lines of the script at moments of great emotional stress are often as stilted and unrealistic as anything in melodrama. Arnold, on hearing of his father's murder, cries out, "Ô crime! hélas, j'expire!" [35] In *La Juive* the shock of Leopold's exposure by Rachel is signalized with "Je frissonne et succombe! Ô jour d'horreur!" [36] And Raoul, at the sight of Valentine whom he mistakenly believes to be false to him, shouts "Trahison! perfidie!" while the crowd answers with "Ciel!" [37]

Such rhetorical expressions are not infrequent; yet, by and large, Scribe's words are prosaic enough not to draw undue attention to themselves. There are no clever discussions, no subtle half-tones, and satire is almost wholly lacking. A greater contrast cannot be imagined than between the colorless quality of these librettos and the vivid language of the romantic drama. "If he tried, no one now could write as bad lines as those of Scribe," said Gautier; [38] but though the criticism was just from a literary point of view, it had small relation to Scribe's work as a librettist. His aim was not to produce pages of fine phraseology any more than it was to draw detailed, full-length character portraits. The one might easily get in the way of the music and the other had best be left to the genius of the composer. Castil-Blaze said that "a maker of operas should restrict himself to saying: 'here are the cavaliers,' or 'the courser departs,'" [39] and to a great extent Scribe followed that prescription. He knew his business well enough to realize that his function should be to give the musician a scaffolding, not a finished building. Hence he kept the bulk of his language neutral and sketched his characters only as silhouettes, concentrating his attention where it mattered the most: on the action.

Scribe's libretti, then, as well as his dramas, are plays of movement, not of character or reflection. Moreover, like the stage works of Alexandre Dumas and the melodrama to which they are so closely related, grand opera is not merely a drama of action, but of spectacular action full of violent turns and stormy irruptions. In a single act of *Les Huguenots* we are shown a tavern scene, a dance interlude, a challenge, a scene of conspiracy, a duel, a street brawl, and finally a marriage procession. While such profusion of movement within a short space of time is by no means the rule in grand opera, this act (III) gives a fair idea of the kind of events one may expect to see there.

Whatever else Scribe's opera books may be, they are not intimate society plays, for the settings alone precluded that. The frame of grand opera is large, and with so much of the action taking place at great public gatherings there is a consequent absence of finesse in its development. Innuendo gives way to bold statement; subtlety is replaced by sharp contrasts. The action tends to hinge on the balance of primitive opposites. It is always a question of life or death for the characters. Fenella can save the man who deceived her at the price of disloyalty to her people; Robert must choose between Good and Evil; Eléazar has to decide between revenge on the Christians and love for his daughter; Rachel may escape her terrible fate by renouncing her religion; and Valentine's choice lies between life with Catholicism and death with her Huguenot lover. Postponement or compromise is strictly ruled out. It is all unashamedly melodramatic, but it is melodrama on the grand scale, gauged to the size of the Opéra and contained in a somewhat tighter and simpler dramatic structure than was customary at the Gaîté or the Ambigu-Comique.

Outside of *Robert le Diable*, Scribe designed plots with definite time limits growing out of the necessities of the action and arrived at with some regard for the personalities involved. That opera, however, runs a course that has much of the serial-like quality of a radio play. Robert, like Hernani or many other characters of melodrama, might easily have continued his adventures indefinitely. His difficulties are finally resolved, it is true, but not through any volition of his own. Right wins out mainly because an arbitrary stopping point has been fixed for the contest. As far as we can tell, Robert might still be wavering uncertainly between his good and his wicked impulses if the powers of Hell had not set a deadline for the decision. The resolution of his destiny by the striking of midnight is of a piece with making Hernani's fate depend on the blast of a horn. Both settlements share the mystery surrounding the origins of the men themselves.

Despite its weaknesses, however, this opera shows at many points how skillfully Scribe organized his material. The introduction of the work, for instance, is a model of its kind. Scribe framed the first act with two large dramatic tableaux, one of which is built around a drinking revel and the second around an equally animated gambling scene. Between these the exposition is massed and the motion of the play is started. As the curtain rises the audience is treated to a conventional, robust chorus during which the spectators have time to get settled and to look at the scenery. The leading characters are then introduced one by one and through them we learn all of their past history that it is necessary to know. Raimbaud, the rustic servitor, tells the story of Robert's origin and early life; while Alice, the simple country maid, relates more family history, symbolizes quite obviously the element of Good as the envoy of the dead mother, and acts the sympathetic sister to whom Robert can pour out the sad tale of his love for the beautiful princess. The preliminaries are completed when Bertram appears on the stage. Alice senses his evil power at once and we are warned of the approaching struggle between the two for the soul of Robert. This is all pure exposition, yet Scribe removed from it any squareness or static quality by distributing the items so that as each is presented it immediately arouses a response in a second person which either furthers the plot or indicates some important trait of character. In that way the past is not merely recited for background purposes but is incorporated into and made the basis for the present action. The librettist has prepared us for whatever is to follow without making it seem as if the material were being handed out from an information booth.

Scribe was always particularly careful to make the opening of an opera as clear as possible. It is usually like the formal introduction to a reception during which the guests are taken around and presented to the house. After that ceremony is finished the action then continues somewhat less rigorously. Scribe made an effort to observe the laws of probability, but one still sees that melodramatic tricks of surprise and concealment figure rather frequently in the process of plot development. Think how much of the subsequent action depends upon Gustave overhearing Amelia's confession of love for him in the fortune teller's booth, or upon Fenella learning of the danger to Alfonso while pretending to sleep, or upon Valentine listening in the shadows while her father plots the murder of Raoul. At these points Scribe was obviously taking the easy way out; but if such artificial aids to locomotion are accepted, the actions may be said to follow a relatively logical course.

Due to the unusual stage facilities of the Académie, however, and to the public's extreme interest in visual display, one need not expect the grand opera librettos to show anything like the simplicity and sobriety of such a piece, say, as Du Roullet's adaptation of the Alceste legend for Gluck's use. While Scribe did not permit his stories to get lost in accessory intrigue, he was always careful to allow place for such relevant divertissements as the action and settings might suggest. The progression of plot is steady but the journey is never so urgent as to rule out pleasure stops on the way. Often, indeed, these are simply concessions to the traditional taste of Paris for spectacle and dancing in its musical theater. In the opening act of *Gustave III*, for example, there is a purely decorative ballet whose sole purpose is to make visible these words of the King:

> Doux charme de ma vie
> Beaux-arts par qui j'oublie
> Les soins de la grandeur.

The danced chorus and "pas de cinq" ballet of act two in *Robert le Diable* also function as part of the scenic background; and almost the entire first half of act two in *Les Huguenots* is nothing but an oversize diversion. All of Scribe's operas, in fact, include rest periods of this kind, but they are not apt to confuse the spectator. His attention is merely relaxed, not led astray. Furthermore, the subsidiary entertainments usually harmonize well enough with the scene to avoid the charge of incongruity pressed by the purists. We may have lost the taste for the divertissements offered here, but we cannot truthfully say that they are so numerous or so obtrusive as to jeopardize seriously the continuity of the action.

The latter was one of Scribe's chief concerns wherever he worked, and at the Opéra it became particularly important to keep the train of the plot clear because of the large number of persons inhabiting his stage. These were not just individuals, for the subject matter he chose to present suggested to him the dramatic use of people in mass. Hence the chorus was allotted a major share in the action. In *La Muette* it represents the populace in revolt; in *La Juive* it is always present as the unthinking, prejudiced enemy of the Jews; and in *Les Huguenots* it takes the roles of the bitterly opposed religious parties. Even in *Robert le Diable* the large ensemble was treated much of the time as an active element in the scene. Since it was an element, however, which obviously did not lend itself to intimate complexities of plot, Scribe was forced to design his actions on large and comparatively simple lines.

His plan of composition, discovered in *La Muette* and used throughout his career at the Opéra, was aimed at effects both of brilliance and of bulk. The operas ordinarily open with a choral scene following which there is a complete exposition presented in such a way that it becomes part of the action. By the end of the first act the movement of the plot is well started and one peak in its course is reached. Thereafter, until the ultimate, spectacular disaster takes place, the play is filled with events of a striking nature which are led in each act through a credible succession of scenes to a massive climax on a crowded stage.[40]

In this scheme of drama nothing is left to the imagination. There is neither intimacy nor ambiguity. Everything is open and expressed, but expressed through action not through language. Realizing that music is a constant threat to the intelligibility of the words, Scribe was never verbose and never allowed an action to be told instead of seen. He believed with Gautier that "any well-made drama must have a skeleton of pantomime," [41] and he arranged his material in a plastic form that would be both clear to the eye and as self-acting as possible. In his productions everything is animated; all is visible and palpable.

One may go further and say that from the standpoint of its architecture, the libretto of Scribe represents primarily an attempt to incorporate spectacle into drama. Scenically, grand opera is a series of vast, panoramic tableaux, and dramatically, it is a succession of massed climaxes culminating in a spectacular dénouement. The connection between the two aspects is vital, for the scenery here is more than mere background: it is rather an environment that determines the scope and furnishes a key to the action. Whereas the literary artist is concerned with words, Scribe began and ended with the scene itself. His work for the Opéra grew out of the contemporary stage; it was not superimposed on it. Accepting as his point of departure the revolutionary developments in the art of the *mise en scène* which had come to the Académie from the popular theaters, he created librettos that reveal a solid welding of spectacle and action.

No better formula could have been devised to satisfy the current requirements of the Académie. The composer was given a libretto that was discreet enough in its language not to interfere with the expansion of the music, that presented a wide variety of picturesque scenes and stirring situations, and that was clearly and skillfully organized in a pattern of movement new to the Opéra. The audience, too, was well served, for a public which regarded "spectacle" and "theater" as synonymous found everything to its taste in the drama of grand opera. The eye was pleased by the brilliance of the settings, and the emotions were roused by the vividness of the action. There was even stimulation for the mind in the subject matter of these pieces, although novelty of theme was carefully softened by conventionality of expression. Responding to the views of the bourgeois society whose spokesman he was, Scribe brought popular drama to the Opéra that was both unique in form and sure in its effect.

VIII

MEYERBEER AND THE OPERA

A s responsibility for the libretto of grand opera rests entirely upon Scribe, so the qualities and defects of its music are concentrated in the person of one man: Meyerbeer. For better or for worse, he unquestionably set the tone for serious French opera music during the whole reign of Louis-Philippe and for a generation afterwards. Like Scribe, he was primarily a man of the theater; but in contrast to the librettist, who was sure of his path almost from the beginning, Meyerbeer did not find his proper bent until he was forty years of age and had made what amounted to the grand tour of musical styles in Europe.

Born in Berlin on September 28, 1791, into a wealthy, cultured Jewish family, he began his career in a serious, scholastic vein which appears to have been too Germanic for the Germans themselves. In any case, his early works received very little support from his countrymen. A moderately successful public debut was made in 1811 with an oratorio entitled *Gott und die Natur*—a work written under the tutelage of the famous Abbé Vogler, one of the most eminent German theorists and teachers of the day. This was followed shortly by an opera, *Jepthas Gelübde,* which failed in Munich, and by *Abimelech,* a two-act comic opera which suffered the same fate in Vienna in 1813. As a pianist Meyerbeer at that time was considered worthy of comparison with the brilliant virtuoso Hummel; but as a composer he evidently was working at variance to the accepted mode of his day. The scholarship and eccentricities of a Vogler, he discovered, could not compete in the German theater with the more sensuous attractions offered by the Italian school of opera. Hence he was inclined to follow the advice of Salieri, the director of the Imperial Chapel in Vienna, who told him in 1816 to go to Italy to see more of the world and to learn how to write for the voice.

Venice was Meyerbeer's first stop and he arrived there when Rossini's *Tancredi* was the rage of the town. It was such a revelation to him that he immediately set himself to modify his own style in accordance with what he had just heard. For two years then he immersed himself again in study, after which he made his Italian debut at Padua with *Romilda e Costanza* (1818). The event turned out so well that he was encouraged to produce *Semiramide ricono-sciuta* the following year in Turin, and in 1820 he brought forth two more works: *Emma di Resburgo* at Venice and *Margherita d'Angiù* at Milan's La Scala, the most important lyric theater in Italy. Meyerbeer, the German composer who had been a failure in his own country, was a success in the native land of opera. Yet after *Il Crociato* (1824), which further increased his reputation, he left the Italian field permanently and gave nothing new to any stage until *Robert le Diable* was produced in Paris seven years later.

It may be that Meyerbeer made the move because he felt he could only repeat himself in Italy;[1] or perhaps he realized that he could never hope to rival Rossini in the latter's own province.[2] We know, at any rate, that as early as 1823 in a letter to the singer, Prosper Levasseur, he expressed a desire to work for the French theater. "I assure you," he said, "that I should consider it a glorious honor to write for the French Opéra. . . . Where but at Paris can one find such immense resources put at the disposal of an artist who wishes to compose truly dramatic music?"[3]

The last sentence gives the real clue to Meyerbeer's change of venue. The pure Italian style in which the flow and pulse of drama stem from the music alone was not for him and he knew it. He Italianized his music as he did his first name but he could not change his nature. Music never ran away with him as it did with Rossini, for his imagination was too literal, too dependent upon stimulus

– 107 –

from without. Meyerbeer, said Dauriac with justice, was one of those artists to whom collaboration was indispensable if their talents were to be brought fully to light.[4] He absorbed enough from Italy to be accepted in its leading theaters, but we may judge from the letter quoted that he understood his destiny lay elsewhere, and that he recognized in his art a basic need for the kind of external dramatic and scenic support that only Paris could offer. Meyerbeer's talent found its proper milieu in France and the French public discovered in him the composer whose ideas of dramaturgy best accorded with their own. The meeting of artist and audience was happy because for both it meant the end of a long quest.

Just how long and how tiresome that search was for the public may be gathered from a glance at the state of music in the Opéra during the two decades preceding Meyerbeer's appearance there. From 1811, when his first piece was performed in Germany, to 1831, when his work finally came to maturity in France, was a period of groping for Meyerbeer as well as for the Académie Royale de Musique. The history of French opera music in those years was, on the whole, anything but spectacular. As *La Revue Musicale* said in 1828: "When one considers the small number of works given by the various administrations during the last twenty years, he is astonished at the activity that formerly reigned in this theater." [5]

The serious French operas produced in that period were neither numerous nor were they often popular. Works such as Méhul's *Les Amazones* (1811) or Cherubini's *Les Abencérages* (1813) fared no better than more ephemeral products like Kreutzer's *Aristippe* (1809), Kalkbrenner's *Oenone* (1812), Reicha's *Natalie* (1816), Berton's *Roger de Sicile* (1817) or Manuel Garcia's *La Mort du Tasse* (1821). In general, Parisians were treated to a series of failures or at best semi-successes most of which were as forgotten a year after their birth as they are today. The one composer who enjoyed any great amount of favor was Spontini, even though his own record was somewhat spotty. *La Vestale,* the fine success of 1807, was followed in 1809 by *Fernand Cortez,* a piece which received a total of only twenty-four performances in its original form, and which, it was said, required "seven years and the horses of Franconi" to reach that figure.[6] After that—leaving aside a two-act occasional work entitled *Pélage ou le Roi de la Paix* (1814), which was written to commemorate the return of Louis XVIII to Paris—Spontini produced only one more opera: *Olympie* (1819), which fell into oblivion after barely a dozen performances.

Despite his setbacks, however, there is little question that the period from 1807 to 1826 belongs to the Italian composer. *La Vestale* received acclaim from the day of its first hearing, and *Fernand Cortez* moved into the permanent repertory after its revision and revival in 1817. Working slowly, revising and correcting, Spontini was universally accepted as the leading composer for the Opéra, although in a sense, of course, his was a victory by default as much as by conquest. Certainly it was not because of the impressive number of his works that he was honored. One unqualified triumph, one belated and considerably lesser success, and one complete failure do not constitute a staggering volume of production. In point of fact, it is so meager that his eminence may seem a little bewildering until we recall the flatness of the surrounding country. Spontini was exceedingly fortunate in his Parisian contemporaries, for at no time until Rossini came to France was he annoyed by competition. He was bothered neither by the tired succession of new works that appeared nor by the scattered revivals of older pieces that took place from time to time.

The taste for these latter had largely been lost and with it went the standards of their production. Gluck's operas were heard occasionally, but the quality of the performances may be judged from the mournful comments of Sophie Leo: "I was really distressed by the affected style in which those divine works *Armida, Alcestis,* and the two *Iphigenias* were offered us by the old company. All was distortion, and an awkward mob of extras in soiled classic costume, their heads wreathed in roses, their faces roughened and bearded, their reddened fists protruding from their coarsely woven sleeves, made an impression as distasteful as it was ridiculous." [7] Other composers received little better treatment. "Monsigny, Philidor, Della Maria, and Grétry had been laid on the shelf . . . for their best compositions were but seldom and then badly produced at the Grand Opéra, where everything was in a lamentable condition." "The Académie Royale de Musique has fallen into such discredit, its receipts have diminished so greatly, its shriekings are held in such horror by everyone, that its most zealous defenders have joined the party of opposition in order to augment the number of mockers." [8]

Even the erection of a new theater in 1821 in the Rue Le Peletier failed to stimulate the public's interest, and by 1824 conditions on the musical stage of Paris were so bad that the energetic Castil-Blaze, who had been one of the most persistent critics of the Opéra, decided to take matters into his own hands. "I wished to change the aspect of our opera, to introduce art in the place of routine." [9] His plan was to present the works of Mozart, Weber, Rossini, and others in translation, and for this purpose he obtained permission to use the Odéon theater. Rossini's *Barber of Seville* (1816) opened the productions of Castil-Blaze on May 6, 1824. Later, the repertory included the same composer's *Otello* and *Tancredi*, Mozart's *Marriage of Figaro* and *Don Giovanni* and Weber's *Der Freischütz*. The original idea was merely to give these foreign operas in French, but in several cases they turned out to be adaptations rather than simple translations. If a piece were not well received the producer was not above doctoring it. Thus, after *Der Freischütz*, or *Robin des Bois* as it was renamed, had been hissed at its performance on December 7, 1824, Castil-Blaze set about its revision—"juggling it according to my own fancy," he said, "in order to fit it to the taste of my auditors." [10] Weber's work then appeared "not in its original beauty, but mutilated, vulgarized, tortured, and insulted in a thousand ways." [11] Going even beyond this liberty, he enlivened his program by presenting an occasional pastiche: a kind of variety show composed of fragments borrowed from the works of several composers. The artistic value of these hodge-podges is indeed slight, yet under such titles as *La Fausse Agnès, Pourceaugnac*, and *La Forêt de Sénart*, they gained more popularity than most of the productions at the Opéra.

The success of the Odéon, taken with the favor shown the Théâtre-Italien since Rossini was called there in 1813, suggested that Paris wanted opera but would not put up with the prevailing drabness of the Acádemie. It was clear that if the latter theater were not to become completely moribund several drastic changes had to be made. To start with, the repertoire needed to be enlarged—not merely by more operas cut on the same pattern as those already on hand, but by fresh works which could stand up to the productions of the Italians. Those few new pieces brought out since *La Vestale* were a sorry and unpopular lot, and the public had shown by its prolonged indifference that it was not attracted any more to the classical French repertory. What had once been strong rivalry between the French and Italian schools was so vitiated by the recent ineptitudes of the former that there was no longer a contest.

The taste for things Italian, especially for Italian music, fostered by Rousseau and the Encyclopedists, championed by Mme. de Staël and Stendhal, officially encouraged by Napoleon, and then carried on by George Sand, Alfred de Musset, Lamartine, Emile Deschamps, and others, reached a climax in Paris following the showing of Rossini's operas at the Théâtre-Italien. These works plus the unchallenged artistry of their interpreters almost completely disposed the public in favor of the Italian style. Lacking anything of its own to offer in competition, the obvious course then for the Opéra was to persuade its greatest rival to come over from the opposing camp. This was done accordingly, and with the commissioning of Rossini to write French works the first big step away from the dismal mediocrity of the recent past was taken.

The reformation of the Opéra's repertory by Rossini began brilliantly on October 9, 1826 with *Le Siège de Corinthe,* an adaptation of his earlier Italian work, *Maometto Secondo* (1820); and continued in 1827 with *Moïse,* a revision of *Mosè in Egitto* (1818), and in 1828 with *Le Comte Ory,* for which Scribe contributed the libretto. In those two years much was accomplished. Under the guidance of Rossini the singing at the Opéra was transformed, and the Italian vocal style was naturalized in the home of the *drame lyrique.* A first-rate composer was working again for the Académie and the change was welcome to critics and audience alike. Looking back on the opening night of *Moïse,* Halévy recalled "the emotion and the raptures of the public." It was, he said, "one of the finest triumphs of music that I have ever witnessed." [12] After suffering so many years of boredom at the Opéra, people revelled in the luxuriant art of the Italian master. "The taste for song is dominant in society," reported

La Revue Musicale; and Rossini, by introducing Italian vocal forms to the French lyric stage, "only yielded to a generally expressed desire." [13] The composer had Paris at his feet. Since he was young and at the height of his powers it seemed likely that he might rule the Opéra for many years to come.

When Auber's opera *La Muette de Portici* was produced in 1828 there still appeared to be no real competition for Rossini. This music is graceful, occasionally scenic, and very restricted in scope. Genre pictures such as the fishermen's chorus in Act II and the market scene in Act III have a wonderful élan quite in the French tradition of those things, and the barcarolles are pleasant on the ear; but Auber's gifts, which showed to great advantage in the lighter vein of *opéra-comique,* were simply not suited by nature to the grand line of musical drama. Whatever its limitations, though, this work was indubitably a success. Even after the monumental scores of *Guillaume Tell, La Juive* and *Les Huguenots,* it was said, there were full houses for the performances of *La Muette.*[14] If its music could not match Rossini's, the piece had other attractions to make up for the lack. For one thing, this was an opera singularly favored by events. Admired at first as a vivid picture of Neapolitan life, *La Muette* very soon developed political overtones which threw into the foreground its scenes of riot and revolt. Appearing as it did on the eve of the July Revolution, it was almost an accessory before that fact, and after the subsequent real-life battles in the streets of Paris, it became a true *pièce de circonstance.*

Much of the enthusiasm for *La Muette,* particularly in and after 1830, no doubt was an expression of revolutionary party spirit, but that still does not wholly account for its success nor does it explain the work's importance in the history of grand opera. Of more significance is the fact that this piece brought popular drama to the lyric theater and reaffirmed in the face of the Rossini cult the traditional taste of Paris for spectacle in its operas. While *Le Siège de Corinthe, Moïse* and *Le Comte Ory* effected a revolution in the mode of singing at the Académie, *La Muette* gave to that stage the first example of what was to become the typical Scribian grand opera libretto and the first complete demonstration of the nineteenth century innovations in décor. Upon these two elements rested the great competitive strength of Auber's opera.

After this it was unlikely that any work written for the French lyric theater could prosper unless it paid heed to the lessons of *La Muette*. Popular, spectacular drama had come to the Opéra and its claims were supported by an overwhelming majority of the public. Only one thing was missing: music which did not neglect what may be termed the "victory of vocalism" so recently won, but which was conceived on a scale big enough to be a true complement to the massive brilliance of the scenes. It remained for Rossini to furnish such a score with *Guillaume Tell* in 1829.

The initial performance of the opera on August 3 of that year was awaited with impatience, and happily the anticipation did not outrun the event. People were first stunned, then wildly enthusiastic in their approval. The writer for *Le Globe* was so overcome by the enormous work that he had difficulty finding words to describe its beauty and power.[15] Gautier said of Rossini that "he is historic . . . from today his name can be placed alongside those of Palestrina, Haydn, Gluck, Mozart, Weber, and Beethoven."[16] All factions of critics and connoisseurs appeared to be satisfied. The story was timely and the setting was attractive. There was action and there was relief in the form of dances and choral interludes. In the music one could find beauty and distinction of melody, consideration for matters of characterization and for dramatic values in general, nicely adjusted and colorful orchestral writing, plus a sure and ample treatment of ensemble groups and choruses. *Guillaume Tell,* in short, was an extraordinary demonstration of how the divergent tastes of Paris could be reconciled and of how the dramatic and scenic assumptions of grand opera could be carried out on a large scale in music.

In view of all these attributes one might reasonably have expected the work to become and to remain the backbone of the Opéra repertory. As a matter of fact, however, its popularity in that period lasted only until the night of November 21, 1831. On that date *Robert le Diable* was presented to Paris, and with the appearance of Meyerbeer under Véron's management the operas of Rossini fell by the wayside or were given only piecemeal at the Académie. Ironically, the man who prepared the public for Meyerbeer thus sealed his own fate.

The primary causes for this sudden shift of leadership are to be found in the invasion of the Opéra by melodrama and in the notable development of stagecraft and design which we have already traced. The scenic brilliance of *La Muette* only whetted people's appetite for more and bigger displays of the decorator's art, and when *Robert* was produced they saw their desires fulfilled. After that event Rossini's "remarkably pure musicality of thought" [17] did not seem so important or so acceptable as it had five years earlier when he was the sole hope of the French lyric stage. The Parisian public, described as one which "asked only to be astonished and surprised" [18] and which "listened to music more with the heels than with the ears" [19] was quick to lionize Rossini in the first flush of appreciation for his work of revitalizing the music at the Opéra; but was equally ready to drop him when a competitor came along who had the talent to use Rossini's contributions and who was willing to accommodate them more fully to the prevailing taste for inflated, spectacular drama.

As far as Rossini's own attitude in the matter is concerned, we know one thing at least for sure: that he wrote no more operas after *Guillaume Tell*. Coming to Paris as a proven master of serious and comic Italian opera, he fell into the current moving toward French grand opera, produced one great work in that pattern and then retired. The fact that he labored on the piece for six months instead of the much shorter time usually spent on his earlier operas possibly indicates that he was aware he had turned in a new direction and needed the extra time to get his bearings. Further, his subsequent refusal to continue in the theater suggests that he came to consider the new path a false one leading away from sound principles of opera construction. At any rate, it is highly unlikely that a man so noted for his fertility of invention should have run out of ideas at the age of thirty-seven. A more reasonable assumption is that he could not or would not go beyond *Guillaume Tell* in his concessions to the gods of melodrama and spectacle. In Rossini's book of opera, music was king. Nothing could be permitted to detract from its sovereign power. [20] Since the rulers and patrons of the Paris Opéra, however, had a different opinion, which was beginning to be shared also at the Théâtre-Italien, the alternatives for Rossini were to compromise his principles or quit. He chose the latter course, becoming thereby what Quicherat called "a casualty of 1830." [21]

The field then belonged to Meyerbeer, wholly and unmistakably. With Cherubini too old to exert any power, Spontini not writing, Rossini retired for reasons of his own, Auber giving the bulk of his time to the Opéra-Comique, and Halévy in essentials a satellite, there is ample justification for considering the scores of Meyerbeer the most complete examples of what we know as "grand opera." Other men wrote for the Académie after 1831, but he set the rules. Berlioz conceded that "Meyerbeer's influence and the pressure exerted by means of his immense fortune, at least as great as that exercised by his *genuine* eclectic talent, on managers, artists, critics, and public as well, make any serious success at the Opéra almost impossible." [22] Accepting the terms that Rossini found intolerable, Meyerbeer joined the forces of the Académie to establish with *Robert le Diable* a form of popular, musico-dramatic spectacle which silenced all competition and which brought its composer a measure of renown virtually unparalleled in the history of the lyric theater.

THE MUSIC OF GRAND OPERA

If one is to assess the music of grand opera properly he must constantly bear in mind the character of the librettos and the settings. Although neither the librettist nor the *metteurs en scène* dictated to the composer what he should write, their creations clearly suggested the style and the formal development of his scores. Once that fact is accepted the musical design becomes more intelligible.

In general, the composer's object was as old as the lyric theater: to maintain as much mobility in the music as possible and still allow himself time to expand his musical ideas. It was an aim followed by the writers of static baroque opera just as by the composers of the eighteenth-century classical school, and it continued to be a goal for those who produced romantic grand opera in the days of Véron. The problem faced by Meyerbeer then was not unusual; but its solution has some original features, outstanding of which is the organization of music into large units of sound corresponding to the dramatic scheme of presenting an action through a series of great tableaux.

Such a plan involved a radical shift in emphasis among the elements comprising the score, and one of the most obvious things to be noticed is the comparatively small place given in grand opera to the developed type of solo song. The aria, that classic halting place in Italian opera, which in the preceding century was normally used dramatically to summarize a situation while expressing a protagonist's state of mind, found itself relegated to a minor position, serving as contrast to weightier matters. Formerly put by choice at the end of a scene where virtuosity had freer rein, it was now more often incorporated into the preliminary action. Characters were seldom placed alone on the stage and granted long soliloquies during which they could indulge in great lyric flights of emotion. There are solo songs in each work but they are not numerous, and it is remarkable how many of these are occupied with narrative and are written in a simple ballad style. In *Robert le Diable* the title part itself contains no full-fledged air, although each of the other main characters was given at least one chance to shine alone. The relative infrequency of such opportunities, however, suggests that in music as in words the individual figures of grand opera lead a decidedly partial life. By the time of *Les Huguenots,* indeed, the concessions to the Italian wing were so reduced that Meyerbeer restricted anything elaborate in solo song to the incidental roles of Marguerite and her page.

The scarcity and the episodic nature of the lyric portions very evidently arose out of the composer's collaboration with a playwright who put his faith in busy plots rich in incidents. Under the circumstances there was naturally a curtailment of operatic lyricism, although we are bound to say that this does not appear always to be a matter for regret. When Halévy settled down to a cavatina, for instance, he was seldom persuasive enough to prevent our thinking "How literate but how dull!" [23] And even Meyerbeer, who had a much greater melodic gift, was usually happier outside the purely lyric sphere. For both composers, however, lyricism was distinctly a side issue, since their music for the most part followed the lead of the drama. That is to say, it is active music in which lyric beauty is secondary to movement. It is music designed especially to color and sharpen the effect of the situations outlined by Scribe without altering their quality; and because of this it shares the limitations of the librettos themselves.

These limitations stem from a reluctance or an inability on the part of either Scribe or Meyerbeer to cut very deeply into the heart of any drama. For all the apparent diversity of action in grand opera one cannot escape the conclusion that its emotional range is small. The scenes change and new combinations of characters appear, but the principal object seems to be to stir up excitement. To further this end much of the action is placed in festive settings where processions and mass conviviality are the rule and where frequent use can be, and is, made of stylized patterns of march and dance origin. As the activity on the stage is mostly of a primary sort putting much emphasis upon visible participation by the characters, so the movement of the music tends to stress the more obvious responses in our nature. It is this which accounts for the serious lack of rhythmic variety that is noticeable in these pieces and which keeps the musical characterizations quite thin and on a somewhat rudimentary level. Scribe created his protagonists as flat surfaces and the composers did little to add to their portraits. Occasionally, it is true, one encounters striking bits of character illumination, but these are rare. The brilliant evocation scene of Act III in *Robert le Diable* during which Bertram appears in all his infernal majesty is one case in point. Another is the final scene in the fourth act of *La Juive* where Eléazar comes vividly to life as both father and Jew as he weighs the fate of Rachel. Ordinarily, however, mere agitation of the characters is substituted for anything more revealing. There is a great deal of vehemence and a considerable amount of two-dimensional eloquence in the musical expression, but there is so little depth that subtle, fully-realized figures are practically out of the question. In place of real psychological penetration we are too often given only the external clatter of a scene.

With the lessening of effort devoted to individual characterization, formerly the chief aim of the lyric theater, the dramatic power in French opera shifted largely from persons to events, and from man as an individual to man as representative of certain social groups or ideas. Rachel is not just a woman in love with Leopold, but a Jewess consorting with a Gentile at a time when such a thing was forbidden. And the lists do not show merely Tell fighting Gesler or Raoul opposing St. Bris, but whole factions or peoples struggling against each other. In music the result was a great thickening of the scores, for the plot was now often carried by the ensembles. The grand trio became almost as much an institution in the French lyric theater as the long solo scene was in Italian opera, yet it was still overshadowed by something bigger. As the individualistic aria gave way to ensemble numbers of one kind or another, i.e. duets, trios, etc., these in turn usually led into or formed a part of larger combinations in which the chorus asserted itself.

The emphasis upon choral work proceeded naturally from a dramatic plan in which individuals represented, or were forced to contend against, large numbers of people. Crowds were obviously essential both to enhance the settings and to carry on the action, but their presence was also desirable for a less artistic reason. They were required because of the very nature of the Académie Royale de Musique. Tradition favored the extensive use of the chorus and sufficient buying power made this possible just as it always had. In Italy, where there was no single state theater and where there were as many kinds of opera as there were large cities, the chorus frequently had been eliminated for reasons of economy. In France, however, where the Opéra had been a government-supported monopoly from the beginning, and where the production of lyric drama was virtually restricted to the capital, the composer could always afford a well-filled stage. Indeed, the glory of the state demanded it.

From Lully's day to Véron's, the chorus thus saw a large amount of service. Still, despite many quite imposing creations, it was service of a limited nature. Its missions were varied yet seldom independent. Lully built his choruses in great vertical masses of consonant harmony described by one critic as "dramatic *ripieni* which enlarge the action and allow it to overflow into the crowd." [24] Rameau, too, followed the same general pattern although his richer musical vocabulary permitted him to write more vividly than his predecessor. Even Gluck did not materially alter the dramatic position of the chorus. He demonstrated during the fine scene at the sacrifice of Orestes in the fourth act of *Iphigénie en Tauride* how a choral body could be used more flexibly in conjunction with recitative and air and still remain within the framework of mythological court opera; but the chorus continued to be a stylized, depersonalized group, occupying a place in French opera similar to the role it filled in the classical Greek drama. While sharing the emotion of a situation it instituted nothing itself.

No heed was paid in France to the Italian classical opera—including the works of Mozart—which envisaged the choral unit as an active body. Choruses became larger after Gluck, but the manner of their employment did not change radically for the next forty years. The Revolution inspired a quantity of enormous hymns and political cantatas; Méhul dreamed of a national festival opera sung by all the inhabitants of Paris divided into choirs of three hundred thousand voices; and composers like Le Sueur, Spontini, and Cherubini responded to the post-revolutionary taste for the grandiose by increasing the apparatus and size of their stage works. At the Paris Opéra, however, the outlines of Gluck were still visible. As far as the chorus was concerned, it was bigger and wore different clothes but its dramatic function was no different from before.[25] Not until *La Muette* cleared the way did it attain the rank of protagonist. Then with fishermen, beggars, tradesmen, and mountaineers where Greek and Roman mobs used to be, the chorus lost its former abstraction and became a vital element of color and life on the stage. Upon receiving the suffrage it ceased being only an hors d'œuvre composed of a collection of supernumeraries, who were far too often ranged on each side of the set like pieces of furniture,[26] and took its place as an important figure in the scene. Instead of reflecting others' movements the chorus became itself a chief participant in the action.

This does not mean of course that individual characters had nothing more to do, nor does it imply that a great mass of singers was always thrusting itself forward on the stage. The producers of grand opera never overlooked the pure scenic value of the chorus, and quite often, in fact, it appeared primarily as part of the background of local color helping to complete the stage picture. That is the case throughout the first act of *La Muette* where the chorus simply contributes to the setting for the wedding celebration of Elvira and Alfonso. It is true also in the fourth act of *Robert le Diable* where the women's chorus sings "Noble et belle Isabelle," in the second act bathers' chorus of *Les Huguenots,* and it is perhaps most evident in the numerous drinking songs and soldiers' revels that occur in all the operas of the time.

Nevertheless, the chorus is most characteristic in grand opera when it is not merely what Edouard Schuré called "a mass that sings," [27] but when it becomes also a mass that acts. Elevation of the choral group to the rank of actor carried with it certain musical obligations, of course, that the composers neither could nor did neglect. With its increased activity the texture of its music became greatly diversified, ranging from unison singing [28] through the ordinary four-part harmonic writing to passages of a more polyphonic nature. Depending on the situation, likewise, the extent of choral engagement varied from short exclamations or exhortations to whole concert pieces. When the chorus simply acted in a secondary or decorative role it was usually sufficient to keep it as harmonic underpinning; but when it became involved directly in the play such treatment obviously was inadequate. The scale of its musical participation had to be raised to the level of its dramatic importance. Hence arose the two fundamentally different ways of using the chorus which may be observed in the first and second act finales of *Robert le Diable*. In the latter instance that group neither is aware of the intrigue nor is vitally concerned in it. Its stage role therefore was limited to taking part in the tournament pageantry, while in music it was restricted to singing an occasional lusty ritornello or to furnishing the choral background for a concertising solo voice. In the first act, however, the large group is engaged in a contest with Robert, expressed musically through a spacious development during which solos, ensembles, and chorus alternate and combine on terms of equality. At this point the choral body truly came into its own, for it was treated musically and dramatically in a dialogued style as plastic and animated as that used for any meeting between individuals.

Pushing a large mass of singers into the foreground in this way naturally presented rather acute problems of stage management. A big chorus is at best an unwieldy unit and unless carefully handled it may very easily produce such a commotion by its actions that the musical effect is smothered. Scribe and Meyerbeer solved this difficulty, however, by adjusting the choral movement and music to the new style of décor designed by Cicéri and Duponchel. The chorus was not constantly on the stage, but it was almost always present and actively involved at the decisive spots in the story. These were the moments eagerly awaited by everyone for they brought together all the resources of the theater. In the master plan of grand opera a climax in the action normally meant an all-hands evolution which came to a peak both scenically and musically. When that high point of drama was reached the movement of the stage resolved itself into a relatively fixed pattern filling in and forming a continuation into the foreground of the scenic tableau. This was then held while the principals, chorus, and orchestra were united in a big musical development designed to top the action and put a broad edge on the emotions of the scene. It was an occasion which depended entirely upon the composer's ability to continue and increase the feeling of tension engendered by the preceding action. The musician then had his inning and he could carry on without being hampered by many of the restrictions that normally must be faced during the course of a work.

These massive developed sections undoubtedly are the chief glory of the Meyerbeerian opera, for they are not only big in volume but big in their structural design. Each is a distinctly outlined segment of the plot, a great wave of action that is arrested for the benefit of the composer at the apex of its forward movement; and each is ordinarily contained in a similarly defined unit of music organized into some kind of large-scale tonal pattern. The conclusion of act one in *Robert le Diable,* for instance, is built in rondo fashion on a sicilienne that opens the scene. Incorporating the complete gambling episode, it carries the action forward until Robert is at swords points with the knights, then freezes that moment of high temper and develops the final appearance of the sicilienne into a brilliant peroration of sound. In the same work the final part of act four is embodied in an extended three-part form with coda, while the waltz and demons' chorus of act three is a full-grown symphonic scherzo. All of these examples demonstrate a definite attempt to link the expression of tonality with the visual and dramatic boundaries of the scene. Wherever one looks, in fact, in the pieces Meyerbeer produced for the Opéra, one finds evidence of a large, formal plan of musical unification that is a direct corollary of the basic dramatic and scenic conceptions advanced by his co-workers.

Of the composers writing for Véron, Meyerbeer alone had the necessary talent and grasp of large-scale form to produce music equal to the scope of the action and to the architectural proportions of the settings. In this matter he was unchallenged either by Auber or by Halévy, the only other men to enjoy success at the Opéra during this period. Auber, himself, was quite unsuited to the grand style for he belonged by training and inclination in the more intimate *opéra-comique*. In *Gustave III* as in *La Muette* he essayed periodically the great climaxes typical of grand opera, but while these sections may approach the volume of a Meyerbeerian conclusion they lack completely its harmonic resourcefulness and its complex organization of vocal and instrumental elements. Auber's scores were merely puffed in size; they did not grow big organically. *La Juive*, on the other hand, has the true feeling of grand opera about it. It is not only large in its dimensions as befits a work by a disciple of Meyerbeer, but it has all the glitter and excitement we associate with that style of lyric drama. In contrast to Auber, Halévy could, as he proved in acts one and three, produce a reasonable facsimile of a Meyerbeerian finale. Significantly, however, it is in such spots where he tried hardest to emulate his master that he is least convincing.

Halévy's real strength did not lie in the expansion of a scene; it rested rather on his ability to catch and illuminate by quick, incisive strokes any sudden turn in the action. At such points he is at his best. One may cite the three occasions in act one of *La Juive* that bring Eléazar into trouble with the crowd, or the pages in act three where Rachel denounces Leopold as he is about to receive Eudora's gift, or the whole of the fifth act finale. The latter example in particular illustrates a working method different from Meyerbeer's. The stage is filled with church dignitaries and with a mob that has just expressed its blood-thirsty desires in a large choral piece which begins "Quel plaisir, quelle joie . . . des Juifs nous serons tous vengés!" Following that, the death sentence is pronounced on the Jews, Rachel takes back her former accusation of Leopold, and then imperiously refuses freedom at the price of giving up her religion. Everything moves quickly, flexibly and decisively. In contrast to previous climaxes which were dwelt on at length, more or less in the style of Meyerbeer, the music here is concise, proceeding without delay towards the cry which ends this last bit of dialogue between Cardinal Brogni and Eléazar:

Brogni: "Ma fille, existe-t-elle encore?"
Eléazar: "Oui!"
Brogni: "Dieu! Où donc est-elle?"
Eléazar: "La voilà!"

As Eléazar triumphantly shouts his last words he points to Rachel who at that moment disappears into the flames. Thus ends one of the most melodramatic scenes in opera—a scene disclosed entirely in a series of sharp thrusts with no extensive musical development either during the action or at its conclusion.

It is not difficult to imagine what Meyerbeer would have done with such a dénouement, nor does it detract from the great success of *La Juive* to suggest that the German composer's method was more typical of Parisian grand opera than Halévy's. If their procedures differed at this point, however, the same cannot be said for the general character of their results. Both men wrote music that is, in the words of Saint-Saëns, like theatrical scenery: "It must not be looked at from too close a distance." [29] The comparison is apt as long as we do not make the mistake of thinking that details of workmanship were neglected or smeared over for the sake of a grandiose effect. What Saint-Saëns probably meant was that this music was written to fit a particular frame, and that some parts which seem overblown or out of focus when read at the piano may be more acceptable if heard in their proper stage setting. The principle involved here is of course cardinal in theatrical art. Without implying that no opera music can sound well divorced from grease paint and scenery, it does mean that some care and a great deal of imagination must be exercised when attempting to judge such music away from its intended locale. Although pure musical values continue to have validity, their force is not absolute. They must constantly be supplemented or even qualified by a consideration of the music's suitability for the dramatic purpose at hand.

Likewise, one cannot disregard the fact that many, if not most, operas have been composed with the possibilities of certain theaters in mind. This was especially true in France, where governmental restrictions had limited severely the number of available outlets. The question of acoustics therefore might well, and in Meyerbeer's case very evidently did, influence the composer's style to a great extent. His music must be viewed as written for large halls and for the Paris Opéra in particular. The character and size of the audience and of the auditorium in which the music was to be performed undoubtedly affected the plans of the authors as they did the thinking of Véron when he wrote that "all the elegance and richness of detail in a score are lost in this immense hall, splendidly lighted and filled with a curious and distracted throng." Here one could be moved only by "grand effects and by broad musical ideas." [30]

Out of the search for the "grand" arose that particular rhetorical quality which is associated with all French serious opera of the time. By "rhetorical" we refer of course only to the general tone of the scores. There was no question whatever, as in Lully's day, of devising a melody according to minute and detailed rules of declamation. In grand opera it was the situation that counted, not the words accompanying it. Hence the composer was less concerned with individual word setting than with emphasizing the essentially grandiloquent nature of the action and the décors. What Scribe said in verse, Meyerbeer proclaimed in music. As the characters were brought into the public square their emotional expression naturally assumed a coarser tone than would be likely in a more intimate setting. They were forced to raise their voices by the very nature of their surroundings.

Yet if the pitch of excitement in grand opera ran high, it did not lead generally to congestion, for Meyerbeer had enough theater sense to realize that continuous eloquence is tiring—that one's attention can best be held by distributing the degrees of intensity through a scene. Act three of *Les Huguenots* with its sprawling profusion of activity and sound may be advanced as an illustration to the contrary, but it is a mistake to take this as typical of Meyerbeer's work. Following immediately upon it, in fact, is an act that is a study in concentrated effectiveness. The first scene, especially, during which St. Bris and his fellow conspirators forge an unholy pact against the Huguenots, is justly celebrated as a high spot in opera construction. Catching the proper undercurrent of sinister suggestion in his orchestra from the beginning, Meyerbeer portrayed masterfully the deadly infection of intolerance and revenge clothed in pious words which gathered momentum until it broke forth with the frenzied cry, "Frappez tous sans relâche! Dieu le veut! Dieu l'ordonne!" It is true that Meyerbeer played his big scenes for all they were worth and sometimes perhaps a bit more, but one must also admit that as a rule each of his massive developments had its genesis in a dramatic situation which was carefully introduced and cultivated until the moment was ripe for it to burst. His largest musical resources were not just tossed about at random any more than hordes of "supers" were merely pulled in by the scruff of the neck to fill a stage on which they really did not belong.

The composer marshalled his vocal forces in accordance with a skillfully designed plan and a similar directing power may be observed in his handling of the orchestra. When one comes to the subject of Meyerbeer and the orchestra he has arrived on familiar ground—so familiar, indeed, that it is scarcely necessary now to catalogue the many new and striking instrumental effects that he devised.[31] Suffice to say that he was in the forefront of those men around 1830 who were engaged in expanding both the size and the expressive range of the instrumental ensemble. The spirit that drove contemporary poets to seek a more vivid and colorful use of language, and that led the artists of the theater to produce their varied and magnificent stage settings, likewise turned the minds of composers to the search for new orchestral sonorities. Precedent for the latter effort had already been set in the operas of Johann Simon Mayr (1763–1845), known throughout Europe for their dramatic and coloristic use of instruments;[32] and from these models Meyerbeer pressed on in the van of a company including Berlioz and later Wagner to develop the more independent and modern treatment of the orchestra.

This was a project that met with the approval of the French public, which had never abandoned itself completely to the attractions of vocalism in the manner of its Italian neighbors;[33] but there were a few individuals who were gravely concerned over what they considered an encroachment on the rights of the singers. The threat to vocal supremacy arising out of the orchestra pit was all too obvious to go unchallenged by the partisans of the classic style in lyric drama. Rossini, despite his own noteworthy contributions to orchestral art,[34] is known to have been alarmed some time before at the popularity of Simon Mayr;[35] and by 1826 the French writer, Ludovic Vitet, felt during the performance of *Le Siège de Corinthe* a "certain inquietude for the future of music, which seems compromised by a frightening luxury of instrumental harmony."[36] Alfred de Musset, too, was shocked at what he termed the "fracas of the orchestra";[37] while H. M. Barton, one of the more conservative composers and critics of Paris, went farther and delivered what is probably the period's most bitter denunciation of the new orchestral role in opera. Pinning his faith to the ideas of the preceding century which for him fixed the rules of musical art, he found that the newcomers had entirely abandoned the route so well traced for them. Purity of style and simplicity of means, he complained, were forgotten in a profusion of accessories, all of which tended to emphasize effect at the expense of dramatic truth. "The mechanical part of the art seems to be everything for them, for the pieces written in the spirit of this new system are rather battles of the orchestra against the singers than true dramatic works; and in this struggle, in accordance with the capital vice of their method, it is the orchestra which almost always wins the palm."[38]

The anxiety voiced by these men was all too justified by later events; but in 1830 it still related more to possibilities than to present actualities. Party though he was to the growth of the orchestra's power in the theater, Meyerbeer on most occasions kept it under control. Even in *Robert le Diable*, where one finds an almost elementary joy in orchestral brilliance, the instruments are usually held in balance with the voices. Meyerbeer's orchestra punctuates, underlines, develops its own ideas, adds color to the scene, does all of the things for which it has been praised. It is seldom quiet; but what is more to the point, it still knows its place. It does not intrude brashly on the singer's province, forcing that poor soul, as in some later operas, to fight his way continually through an engulfing mass of instrumental sound; because neither Meyerbeer nor his colleagues at the Académie ever quite came to think that the main action of the play had shifted to the pit. That aberration was reserved for the late nineteenth-century German music-drama. Although arias were scarcer than before, the vocal parts in grand opera still had an amplitude and a continuity which prevented them falling into an incidental position in relation to the instruments.

To this extent, Meyerbeer kept his lines of communication open to the practice of eighteenth-century classical opera. Beyond that, however, the connection was dead. The composer was writing for a later generation and his chief ties were with his own day. Few indeed have ever had a livelier sense of the moment or a keener understanding of their audience. "He is the man of his time," said Heine, "and the time which always knows how to choose its men has raised him with a tumult on the shield." [39] Following in the line of the Académie's foreign-born leaders which included Lully, Gluck, Spontini and Rossini, Meyerbeer rose to a commanding position in Paris because he appeared able to express the musical desires of the opera public better than the French composers themselves. "If no other success of our day equals his," observed Henri Blaze de Bury, it is because he, "more clearly than anyone else, divined our instincts, comprehended our sympathies, and in a word established himself in the domain of our national music." [40]

In the eyes of certain German compatriots Meyerbeer thus relinquished any claim to citizenship in the community of honest artists. To Weber he was a musician of ability but a renegade who had deserted the musical faith of his fatherland for foreign idols. Schumann put a low estimate on his work saying: "In *Il Crociato* I still counted Meyerbeer among musicians; in *Robert le Diable* I began to have my doubts; in *Les Huguenots* I place him at once among Franconi's circus people." [41] Mendelssohn found his music "frigid and heartless"; [42] and Wagner wrote in his most vitriolic manner that Meyerbeer was nothing but a vulgar dispenser of senseless "effects," and that in his music there is shown "so appalling an emptiness, shallowness and artistic nothingness, . . . we are tempted to set down his specific musical capacity at zero." [43]

To all these barbs of criticism from abroad Meyerbeer offered no rebuttal. He needed none, for the clamorous reception given his works in Paris rendered any defense superfluous. The *Moniteur Universal* praised his style, "distinguished by simplicity, verve and force." [44] George Sand looked upon him as a "great dramatic poet." [45] Balzac described *Robert le Diable* as a faithful reflection of the heroic life during the Age of Chivalry; [46] while Berlioz said that the music of *Les Huguenots* was "stamped with grandeur and truth." [47] Meyerbeer was writing for France, not for his German confrères, and he realized clearly the difference. It was not a question of discarding everything he had learned in Germany or in Italy, but of incorporating that knowledge into a style which fitted the dimensions and the intellectual tone of the Académie Royale de Musique.

Shaping his work to the particular character of this stage, he produced scores that have the color and the massive architecture of the settings plus the broad popular nature of the drama. As he stiffened the formal structure of grand opera he also widened its emotional base so that his music became, as Heine said, rather social than individual. Wagner, himself, in an unguarded moment acknowledged after *Les Huguenots* that Meyerbeer introduced in the lyric theater a style "full of grandeur and simplicity which enjoyed the infinite advantage of having its roots in the heart and ears of the people." [48] This unexpected tribute is not off the mark if "people" is taken to mean the bourgeois society for whom the composer of grand opera wrote. Possessing neither the poetry of Schumann nor the fire of Berlioz, Meyerbeer was a true bourgeois Prometheus—a man who knew both his métier and his public, and who created an art that was expertly adapted to the world of his day. If his fame is now as faded as that of Scribe, Meyerbeer nevertheless occupies a secure niche in operatic history, for he not only gave a definitive style to the musical theater of Romanticism but taught something to all the opera composers of the century about the use of the orchestra and about the dramatic construction of large-scale scenes in music. [49]

IX

EPILOGUE

THE SYSTEMATIC planning that governed every detail of its production is ample refutation of any idea that grand opera was a slap-dash concoction thrown together overnight. Since its creators, however, were not only men of unusual talent and skill but also confirmed opportunists who took their fortune where it could be found, they stood apart from the endless swirl of theory and controversy that invariably accompanied dramatic and operatic production in France. French Romantic drama had its articles of doctrine, and even melodrama was furnished a body of aims and beliefs by Pixérécourt; but neither Scribe nor Meyerbeer ever went to the trouble to publish an explanation or defense of their procedures. Véron alone was interested in telling at any length what he thought a work designed for the Académie should contain, and his summary was written many years after he resigned from the theater. Also, it is more a statement of administrative policy than of ideal principle.

"An opera in five acts," he said, "cannot exist without a very dramatic action which exposes the grand passions of the human heart and which brings powerful historical interests into play. This dramatic action, however, must be as intelligible to the eyes as the movement of a ballet. It is also necessary that the chorus be given a lively role and that it becomes, so to speak, one of the characters engaged in the piece. Each act should offer contrasts of decorations, of costumes, and especially of cleverly prepared situations. . . . When one has at his command a vast theater . . . with an orchestra of more than eighty musicians, nearly eighty choristers, men and women, eighty figurants without counting the children, and a crew of sixty machinists to handle the decorations, the public awaits and demands great things of you. You fail in your mission if so many resources are used merely in the service of comic operas or *vaudevilles*." [1]

Véron's account is not only a fair description of the 1830 style in serious French opera, but is also unequivocal evidence of the thorough-going practicality of its conception. As Wagner remarked: "Paris is the only city in the world where such pieces alone are performed as have been expressly written and accurately calculated for the boards on which they reach portrayal." [2] Spending no time outlining their theoretical aims, the authors of grand opera arrived empirically at their distinctive union of spectacle, drama, and music after carefully assaying the available means of production and molding them to the conditions and desires of the Académie's audience. This variety of musical theater had its origin, one may say, in the market place, under the influence of no single code of esthetics but alive to any ideas that had strength enough to gain currency in the world at large. Lacking the support of a literary or musical coterie, it was as sensitive to public opinion and almost as dependent upon popular approval as any melodrama of the Boulevard.

The total result, in the judgment of Alfred de Musset and of others who preferred opera in the Italian vein, was "a false, affected and ridiculous genre" based on a system of perpetual exaggeration; [3] but in the eyes of the great public it was art of the highest order, worthy of all honor and support. To a bourgeois society that had lost all contact with the past glories of the French lyric theater and that had shown itself singularly unable to appreciate the finely-modeled, individualistic style of a Mozart or of a Rossini at his best, grand opera of 1830 came as a revelation. Seasoning originality with compromise, it spoke to its auditors in a language they could understand. While the older aristocracy took its patronage to the Théâtre-Italien, the bourgeoisie stormed the doors of the Académie Royale de Musique, for there they found an art made in their own image—an art that was at once revolutionary and reassuring, that extended one hand towards Romanticism as it held fast to conventionality with the other. Grand opera's luxury, size, and complete seriousness gave it an appearance of greatness which was both stimulating and flattering to its audience; yet there was always enough commonness in its expression to keep it easily accessible. Tied to no program, either classic or romantic, it was in all essentials a popular art keyed to the tempo and taste of its day.

Carried on an unprecedented wave of public approval, grand opera became a financial success that exceeded the most sanguine hopes of its producers and a triumph of style whose influence reached wherever lyric drama was played. As it shook off its lassitude of the past twenty years the Opéra once again asserted itself as the official seat of French musical life. Paris, which gave only meager support to lieder, chamber music, or the symphony, lavished its attention on the lyric stage. There, observed Joseph d'Ortigue, "were concentrated all the interests of art." [4] There, too, we find the commercial center of music—not just for Paris, but for Europe. As the Académie regained its prestige the geographical range of its influence was extended. Musicians of talent from all over the Continent turned more and more to Paris for recognition and fortune and less to Vienna or Dresden or Milan. Thanks to the happy artistic collaboration of Scribe, Meyerbeer, and their scene designers, and to Véron's uncommon ability as a business executive and promoter, Paris found itself in the early 1830's well on the way towards becoming the acknowledged world-capital of opera.

"With very few exceptions," admitted Wagner, "among which only the first opera houses of Italy can be included, there is no original theater but that of Paris. All the rest are merely its copies." [5] At no period in its history, in fact, did the French lyric drama play a larger role than during the middle fifty years of the nineteenth century. Grand opera's characteristic plot design, its variety of orchestral treatment, and its dramatic emphasis of huge, symphonically developed tableaux were elements that made their mark on all branches of the lyric theater. French writers of opera were completely dominated by the Meyerbeer-Scribe formula; among many other Italian composers, Verdi himself submitted to its influence in most of his works up to *Aïda* (1871); while Wagner, who professed the most implacable hatred for grand opera, not only curried favor with Meyerbeer and sought a libretto from Scribe after their first joint success, but followed their principles in early works such as *Rienzi* (1838–1840) and the *Flying Dutchman* (1841) and quite evidently turned to profit their system of musico-dramatic unification when he expanded later his own ideas of the *Gesamtkunstwerk*. As a matter of fact, the final scene in *Die Meistersinger* is still a typical grand opera tableau.

Grand opera thus spread over the world, but though it acquired an international significance it remained undeniably French in its conception; and it did so primarily because of the peculiar importance it attached to the whole question of optical effect. Recognizing the visual as well as the aural demands of the spectator, the Académie Royale de Musique once more confirmed its original practice whose aim, according to an eminent seventeenth-century critic, was to "give equal pleasure to the eyes and to the ears." [6] The lyric drama of 1830 was a far cry from that heard in the days of Louis XIV, but in its attempt to unite tableaux and music into a superorganism of spectacle and sound it might well adopt those words of La Bruyère as its motto.

Upon this basis Meyerbeer and Scribe collaborated with the scenic artists of the Académie to create that "complex and multiple style" of musical theater whose success, as Emile Deschamps said, lay in "the accord, the fusion of all elements in just proportions." [7] Displaying neither the exuberant musical nature of the Italian school nor the dominant literary strain of the Lully tradition, grand opera in a very real sense was a compound work resting upon the joint efforts of dramatist, musician and *metteurs en scène*. Guided by no *a priori* system of esthetics but following, nevertheless, a consistent line of action, these men pooled their talents to produce a form of lyric drama that resumed the chief tendencies of its day, that completely satisfied the wishes of the bourgeois public for which it was designed, and that won a brilliant place in nineteenth-century life both as an art and as a business.

NOTES

CHAPTER 1

1. Paul H. Láng, *Music in Western Civilization* (New York, 1941), p. 736.

2. Eugène Scribe, *Œuvres complètes* (Paris, 1899), *Le Mariage d'Argent,* I, iii, 306–307.

3. Véron entitled his autobiography: "Mémoires d'un bourgeois de Paris."

4. *The King's Henchman* by Deems Taylor and *Merry Mount* by Howard Hanson testify that its influence reaches even to the present day.

CHAPTER 2

1. Frederick B. Artz, *Reaction and Revolution 1814–1832* (New York, 1934), p. 30.

2. Arsène Houssaye, *Les Confessions* (Paris, 1885), I, 399.

3. Artz, *op. cit.,* p. 270.

4. Lucas-Dubreton, *La Royauté bourgeoise* (Paris, 1930), p. 21.

5. Louis Marie Quicherat, *Adolphe Nourrit* (Paris, 1867), I, 87.

6. Georges Bureau, *Le Théâtre et sa législation* (Paris, 1898), p. 61.

7. *Encyclopédie de la musique et dictionnaire du Conservatoire* (Paris, 1920–1931), Part II, VI, 3764.

8. Paul Pelissier, *Histoire administrative de l'Académie Nationale de Musique et de Danse* (Paris, 1906), p. 35.

9. Pierre Bossuet, *Histoire administrative des Rapports des théâtres et de l'Etat* (Paris, 1909), p. 151.

10. Raymond de Pezzer, *L'Opéra devant la loi et la jurisprudence* (Paris, 1911), p. 23.

11. *Encyclopédie de la Musique*, Part II, VI, 3773.

12. *Ibid.*, pp. 91 f.

13. Castil-Blaze, *L'Académie Impériale de Musique* (Paris, 1885), II, 27.

14. Pezzer, *op. cit.*, p. 26.

15. Pelissier, *op. cit.*, p. 102.

16. Pezzer, *op. cit.*, p. 29.

17. Bossuet, *op. cit.*, p. 156.

18. Pezzer, *op. cit.*, pp. 30 f.

19. Castil-Blaze, *op. cit.*, II, 200.

20. *Ibid.*, II, 189.

21. *Ibid.*, II, 200.

22. Théophile Gautier, *Mademoiselle de Maupin* (Paris, 1834), *Préface*.

23. Bossuet, *op. cit.*, p. 157.

24. Louis Véron, *Mémoires d'un bourgeois de Paris* (Paris, 1856–1857), III, 102.

25. *Cahier des charges de la direction de l'Opéra en régie intéressée*, February 28, 1831, quoted in Véron, *Mémoires*, III, 107.

26. Castil-Blaze, *op. cit.*, II, 200.

27. Article 9 of Véron's *Cahier des charges* required the production each year of the following new works: 1 grand opera in 3 or 5 acts, 1 major ballet, 2 small operas in 1 or 2 acts, and 2 small ballets. Quoted in Véron, *op. cit.*, III, 107.

28. The Decree of Louis-Philippe dated August 24, 1831, stated that: "The dispositions of the Decree of August 13, 1811, relative to a tax for the benefit of the Académie Royale de Musique, shall cease to be in effect." Quoted in Véron, *op. cit.*, III, 102.

29. Article 4 of Véron's *Cahier des charges*, quoted in Véron, *op. cit.*, III, 107.

30. Lucas-Dubreton, *op. cit.*, p. 16.

CHAPTER 3

1. Louis Véron, *Mémoires d'un bourgeois de Paris* (Paris, 1856–1857), III, 105.

2. *Ibid.*, III, 104–105.

3. Auguste Ehrhard, "L'Opéra sous la direction Véron," *Revue Musicale de Lyon,* Année 5 (1907), 45.

4. Véron, *op. cit.*, I, 2.

5. Hippolyte Castille, "Les Hommes et les mœurs sous le règne de Louis-Philippe," *Revue de Paris,* August 1, 1853, p. 445.

6. Louis J. Arrigon, *Les Années romantiques de Balʒac* (Paris, 1927), p. 88.

7. Arsène Houssaye, *Les Confessions* (Paris, 1885), II, 285.

8. Heinrich Heine, *Über die Französische Bühne, Vertraute Briefe an August Lewald,* Vol. VI of *Sämtliche Werke* edited by Fritz Strich (Munich, 1925), 10th Letter.

9. Horace de Viel-Castel, *Mémoires* (Paris, 1883), I, 480.

10. Charles P. Séchan, *Mémoires d'un homme de théâtre* (Paris, 1883), p. 190.

11. *Ibid.*

12. Charles de Boigne, *Petits mémoires de l'Opéra* (Paris, 1857), p. 6.

13. Jacques Boulenger, *Les Dandys* (Paris, 1932), p. 135.

14. Viel-Castel, *op. cit.*, I, 48.

15. *Ibid.*, I, 180.

16. *Ibid.*, I, 181.

17. Boulenger, *op. cit.*, p. 132.

18. *Ibid.*

19. Henri A. B. Loustalan, *La Publicité dans la presse française* (Paris, 1933), pp. 11–19.

20. Véron, *op. cit.*, III, 49.

21. Comte Edmond D'Alton-Shée, *Mes mémoires* [1826–1848] (Paris, 1869), I, 65.

22. *La Revue de Paris,* XII (1834), 308.

23. Arsène Houssaye, *op. cit.*, II, 274.

24. Henry F. Chorley, *Music and Manners in France and Germany* (London, 1844), II, 256.

25. Heinrich Heine, *Luteʒia,* Vol. IX of *Sämtliche Werke* (Munich, 1925), Part II, LV, 272.

26. Viel-Castel, *op. cit.*, I, 193.

27. Ehrhard, *op. cit.*, pp. 179–180.

28. Charles Maurice, *Histoire anecdotique du théâtre* (Paris, 1856), II, 124, letter of August 11, 1835.

29. *Ibid.*, II, 89, letter of May 4, 1834.

30. *Ibid.*, II, 176, letter of February 5, 1838.

31. *Ibid.*, I, 368, letter of January 26, 1826.

32. Véron, *op. cit.*, III, 133.

33. *Ibid.*, III, 134.

34. Houssaye, *op. cit.*, II, 274.

35. *Ibid.*, II, 275.

36. Véron, *op. cit.*, III, 191.

37. *Ibid.*, III, 145.

38. *Ibid.*, III, 146.

39. Alphonse Royer, *Histoire de l'Opéra* (Paris, 1875), p. 128.

40. Albert de Lasalle, *Les Treize Salles de l'Opéra* (Paris, 1875), p. 238.

41. Adolphe Jullien, *Paris dilettante au commencement du siècle* (Paris, 1884), p. 168.

42. Véron, *op. cit.*, III, 114–115.

43. Mme. Emile de Girardin, *Lettres Parisiennes* (Paris, 1868), I, 91–93, 6th letter dated March 15, 1837.

44. Eugène Briffault, "L'Opéra," *Le Livre des Cent-et-Un* (1834), XV, 374–375.

45. J. Lucas-Dubreton, *La Royauté bourgeoise* (Paris, 1930), p. 24.

46. Véron, *op. cit.*, V, 320.

47. Lucas-Dubreton, *op. cit.*, p. 7. Remark attributed to Louis-Philippe when he was still the Duc d'Orléans.

48. Séchan, *op. cit.*, p. 217.

49. Maxime du Camp, *Souvenirs littéraires* (Paris, 1892), I, 39.

50. *Encyclopédie de la musique et dictionnaire du Conservatoire* (Paris, 1920–1931), Part II, VI, 3767.

51. Séchan, *op. cit.*, p. 183.

52. Marcel Bouteron, *Danse et musique romantiques* (Paris, 1927), p. 58.

53. Briffault, *op. cit.*, p. 385.

54. Castille, *op. cit.*, p. 435.

55. Ehrhard, *op. cit.*, p. 208.

56. Séchan, *op. cit.*, p. 183.

57. Castille, *op. cit.*, p. 436.
58. J. T. Merle, *Du Marasme dramatique en 1829* (Paris, 1829), p. 6.
59. Briffault, *op. cit.*, p. 372.
60. Chorley, *op. cit.*, I, 6.
61. IV (1831), 113.
62. De Boigne, *op. cit.*, p. 303.
63. Arrigon, *op. cit.*, pp. 183–185.
64. Briffault, *op. cit.*, pp. 382–384.
65. *La Mode, Revue du Monde Elégant*, XVIII (1834).
66. *L'Artiste*, IX (1835), 292.
67. Véron, *op. cit.*, III, 231.
68. Viel-Castel, *op. cit.*, I, 177.
69. Castille, *op. cit.*, p. 443.

Chapter 4

1. Henry F. Chorley, *Music and Manners in France and Germany* (London, 1844), I, 17–20.
2. Hector Berlioz, *Mémoires* (Paris, 1878), I, 329 f.
3. Henri Blaze de Bury, *Meyerbeer et son temps* (Paris, 1857), p. 48.
4. Charles de Boigne, *Petits mémoires de l'Opéra* (Paris, 1865), p. 70.
5. *Ces Demoiselles de l'Opéra* (Paris, 1887), p. 140.
6. De Boigne, *op. cit.*, p. 42.
7. Alphonse Royer, *Histoire de l'Opéra* (Paris, 1875), p. 129.
8. Paul Scudo, *Critique et littérature musicales* (Première Série, Paris, 1856), p. 310.
9. Sophie Leo, "Musical Life in Paris (1817–1848)," a chapter from *Erinnerungen aus Paris* (Berlin, 1851), translated by Oliver Strunk, *The Musical Quarterly*, XVII (1931), 261.
10. *La Revue Musicale*, I (1827), 99.
11. Royer, *op. cit.*, p. 158.
12. *La Revue Musicale*, I (1827), 101.
13. De Boigne, *op. cit.*, p. 12.
14. *Ibid.*, p. 110.
15. Jacques Fromentin Halévy, *Derniers souvenirs et portraits* (Paris, 1863), p. 142.

16. *Ibid.*, p. 145.

17. Louis Marie Quicherat, *Adolphe Nourrit; sa vie, son talent, son caractère, sa correspondance* (Paris, 1867), I, 39.

18. Blaze de Bury, *op. cit.*, p. 83.

19. Chorley, *op. cit.*, I, 67.

20. Louis Véron, *Mémoires d'un Bourgeois de Paris* (Paris, 1856–1857), III, 180.

21. Blaze de Bury, *op. cit.*, p. 87.

22. Halévy, *op. cit.*, pp. 156–157.

23. *Ibid.*, p. 151.

24. *Ibid.*, p. 145.

25. De Boigne, *op. cit.*, p. 75.

26. Maxime du Camp, *Souvenirs littéraires* (Paris, 1882), I, 122.

27. Blaze de Bury, *op. cit.*, p. 98.

28. Royer, *op. cit.*, pp. 160–161.

29. Blaze de Bury, *op. cit.*, p. 99.

30. Eugène Briffault, "L'Opéra," *Livre des Cent-et-Un*, XV (1835), 373.

31. Scudo, *op. cit.*, p. 310.

32. *La Revue Musicale*, I (1827), 99.

33. Castil-Blaze, *L'Académie Impériale de Musique* (Paris, 1855), II, 43.

34. Royer, *op. cit.*, p. 135.

35. Blaze de Bury, *op. cit.*, p. 86.

36. *Ibid.*, p. 87.

37. *La Revue Musicale*, IV (1829), 332.

38. Charles de Boigne, *op. cit.*, p. 86.

39. Véron, *op. cit.*, III, 325.

40. De Boigne, *op. cit.*, p. 87.

41. *Ibid.*, p. 88.

42. Véron, *op. cit.*, III, 237.

43. *Ibid.*, III, 236.

44. Berlioz, *op. cit.*, II, 91.

45. Théophile Gautier, *Histoire de l'art dramatique en France* (Paris, 1858), I, 191.

46. De Boigne, *op. cit.*, p. 86.

47. De Boigne, *op. cit.*, p. 91.

48. Théophile Gautier, *Histoire de l'art dramatique en France* (Paris, 1858), I, 192 f.

49. Véron, *op. cit.*, III, 240.

50. Philarète Chasles, *Mémoires* (Paris, 1877), II, 14.
51. Gautier, *Histoire du romantisme* (Paris, 1895), p. 113.
52. *La Revue de Paris*, June, 1831, p. 251.
53. De Boigne, *op. cit.*, p. 8.

CHAPTER 5

1. Louis Véron, *Mémoires d'un bourgeois de Paris* (Paris, 1856–1857), III, 256–257.
2. Théophile Gautier, *Histoire de l'art dramatique en France* (Paris, 1858), III, 146.
3. Gustave Planche, "Histoire et Philosophie de l'Art," *Revue des Deux Mondes*, IV (1834), 542–543.
4. *L'Artiste*, VIII (1834), 289.
5. Mme. Emile Girardin, *Lettres Parisiennes* (Paris, 1868), I, 95.
6. *L'Artiste*, *loc. cit.*
7. Until October 13, 1831, the date of the first performance of Auber's *Le Philtre*, the Opéra curtain remained up for the entire length of a work and all changes of scenery were made in full view of the audience.
8. Cf. S. Wilma Holsboer, *Histoire de la mise en scène dans le théâtre français de 1600 à 1657* (Paris, 1933).
9. Marie Antoinette Allévy, *La Mise en scène en France dans la première moitié du dix-neuvième siècle* (Paris, 1938), 10.
10. Emile Perrin, "Etude sur la Mise en Scène," *Les Annales du Théâtre et de la Musique* (1882), VIII, 32.
11. *Ibid.*, 18.
12. Houdar de Lamotte, "Discours à l'Occasion des Macchabées," *Les Paradoxes littéraires de Lamotte*, collected and edited by B. Jullien (Paris, 1859), 450–451.
13. Denis Diderot, "De la poésie dramatique," *Diderot's Writings on the Theater*, edited by F. C. Green (Cambridge, 1936), pp. 188 ff.
14. See Voltaire, *Lettre à M. Dumarsais*, October 12, 1755, in *Œuvres Complètes* (Paris, 1859), XI, 754.
15. Beaumarchais, *Un Essai sur le drame sérieux* (Paris, 1767), p. xxviii.
16. Pierre J. B. Nougaret, *De l'art du théâtre en général* (Paris, 1769), pp. 337–339.

17. Guilbert de Pixérécourt, "Derniers réflexions de l'auteur sur le mélodrame," *Théâtre choisi de G. de Pixérécourt* (Nancy, 1843), IV, 493 ff.

18. Louis G. A. De Bonald, *Mélanges* (third edition, Paris, 1852), pp. 403–404.

19. J. F. Mason, *The Melodrama in France from the Revolution to the Beginning of Romantic Drama* (Baltimore, 1912), p. 147.

20. *Ibid.*, p. 141.

21. Allévy, *op. cit.*, pp. 43–44.

22. Julien Louis Geoffroy, *Cours de littérature dramatique* (second edition, Paris, 1825), VI, 157.

23. "Daguerre," in *Biographie universelle* (Paris, 1852), Vol. X.

24. "Daguerre," in *Grand Dictionnaire universel du XIXe siècle* (Paris, 1870), Vol. VI.

25. Patented in 1787, the Argand lamp has a tubular wick which admits a current of air inside as well as outside the flame. Named after its Swiss inventor, Aimé Argand, of Geneva.

26. *Ibid.*

27. *Almanach des spectacles* (Paris, 1823), p. 240.

28. Gautier, *op. cit.*, II, 174–175.

29. Allévy, *op. cit.*, p. 75.

30. Alexandre Dumas, *Souvenirs dramatiques* (Paris, 1881), I, 394.

31. Charles Séchan, *Souvenirs d'un homme de théâtre* (Paris, 1855), p. 11.

32. Emile Perrin, "Etude sur la Mise en Scène," *Les Annales du Théâtre et de la Musique* (Paris, 8th Année [1822]), p. 3.

33. A. J. J. Deshayes, *Idées générales sur l'Académie Royale de Musique* (Paris, 1822), p. 8.

34. Jean T. Merle, *De l'Opéra* (Paris, 1827), pp. 32–33.

35. Albert de Lasalle, *Les Treize Salles de l'Opéra* (Paris, 1875), p. 243.

36. Alphonse Royer, *Histoire de l'Opéra* (Paris, 1875), p. 184.

37. Heinrich Heine, *Über die französische Bühne, Vertraute Briefe an August Lewald,* Vol. VI of *Sämtliche Werke* (Munich, 1925), 10th Letter.

38. Arthur Pougin, *Le Théâtre à l'Exposition de 1889* (Paris, 1890), p. 32.

39. Allévy, *op. cit.*, p. 52.

40. Henri Bouchot, *Le Luxe français: La Restauration* (Paris, 1893), p. 314.

41. Jacques F. Halévy, *Derniers souvenirs et portraits* (Paris, 1863), p. 154.

42. *La Revue Musicale*, III (1828), 135.

43. Eugène Briffault, "L'Opéra," *Paris ou le Livre des Cent-et-Un* (1835), XV, 374.

44. Perrin, *op. cit.*, p. 61.

45. *Le Journal de Débats*, November 23, 1831.

46. *La Revue des Deux Mondes*, IV (1831), 539.

47. Véron, *op. cit.*, III, 51–52.

48. "Aux ruines de Montfort-l'Amaury," *Odes et Ballades*, Ode XVIII, Livre V (1819–1828).

49. Séchan, *op. cit.*, p. 11.

50. *Le Constitutionnel*, November 23, 1831.

51. Paul Scudo, *L'Année musicale* (Paris, 1860), Première Année, p. 3.

52. *L'Artiste*, VI (1834), Série I, p. 11.

53. *Le Temps*, March 4, 1833.

54. Castil-Blaze, *L'Académie Impériale de Musique* (Paris, 1855), II, 238.

55. *Le Temps*, March 4, 1833.

56. Charles de Boigne, *Petits Mémoires de l'Opéra* (Paris, 1857), p. 73.

57. Jean B. M. A. Challamel, *Album de l'Opéra* (Paris, 1845), p. 18.

58. *Le Courrier Français*, February 27, 1835.

59. *Ibid.*

60. Théophile Gautier, *Les Beautés de l'Opéra* (Paris, 1845), p. 3.

61. *Le Constitutionnel*, February 25, 1835.

62. *Le Temps*, February 26, 1835.

63. Albert Le Roy, *L'Aube du théâtre romantique* (Paris, 1904), pp. 92–93.

64. Jules Janin, *Histoire de la littérature dramatique* (Paris, 1854), VI, 88.

65. Planche, *op. cit.*, p. 542.

66. Louis de Bonald, *Mélanges* (third edition, Paris, 1852), p. 401.

67. Letter from Delacroix to Adolphe Nourrit, quoted in Adolphe Jullien, *Musique* (Paris, 1896), p. 166.

68. Castil-Blaze, *op. cit.*, II, 207.

69. Castil-Blaze, *Sur l'opéra français: Vérités dures, mais utiles* (Paris, 1856), p. 5.

70. *Ibid.*, p. 56.

71. Castil-Blaze, *L'Académie Impériale de Musique* (Paris, 1855), II, 227.

72. Louis M. Quicherat, *Adolphe Nourrit* (Paris, 1867), I, 177.

73. Paul Scudo, *De l'influence du mouvement romantique sur l'art musical et du rôle qu'a voulu jouer M. H. Berlioz* (Paris, 1846), p. 10.

74. *L'Artiste*, IX (1835), 292.

75. Théophile Gautier, *Portraits contemporains* (third edition, Paris, 1874), pp. 341–342.

76. Gautier, *Histoire de l'art dramatique en France* (Paris, 1858), II, 67.

77. *Ibid.*, II, 67.

78. Henry F. Chorley, *Music and Manners in France and Germany* (London, 1844), I, 45.

CHAPTER 6

1. Hippolyte Parigot, *Le Drame d'Alexandre Dumas* (Paris, 1898), p. 161.

2. Neil Cole Arvin, *Eugène Scribe and the French Theater* (Cambridge, 1924), p. 38.

3. *Ibid.*, p. 8.

4. Hippolyte Parigot, *Le Théâtre d'hier* (Paris, 1893), pp. x–xi.

5. Théophile Gautier, *Histoire du romantisme* (Paris, 1895), p. 31.

6. *Ibid.*, p. 25.

7. Preface to *Cromwell*.

8. Gautier, *Histoire du romantisme*, Ch. 11.

9. J. T. Merle, *Du Marasme dramatique en 1829* (Paris, 1829), p. 9.

10. Preface to *Cromwell*.

11. *Chatterton* (1836).

12. Brander Matthews, *French Dramatists of the Nineteenth Century* (New York, 1901), p. 91.

13. See Raymond Leslie Evans, *Les Romantiques français et la musique* (Paris, 1934).

14. The French public did not take kindly to the other provinces of music, and it was not until well towards the middle of the nineteenth century that concert life—begun by Liszt, Thalberg and the

other great virtuosos of the day—assumed the complexion it had acquired in Central Europe many years earlier.

15. Evans, *op. cit.*, p. 142.

16. George Brandes, *Main Currents in Nineteenth Century Literature* (New York, 1904), V, 352.

17. *Le Globe*, 5 March 1828.

18. *La Revue Musicale*, 1830, VI, 40.

19. Louis Véron, *Mémoires d'un bourgeois de Paris* (Paris, 1856–1857), III, 182.

20. *Ibid.*

CHAPTER 7

1. Abbé François Raguenet, *Parallèle des italiens et des français en ce qui regarde la musique et les opéras* (Paris, 1702) p. 6.

2. *René Guiet, L'Evolution d'un genre: Le livret d'opéra en France de Gluck à la révolution*, "Smith College Studies in Modern Languages" (Northampton, 1936–1937), XVIII, p. 16.

3. Abbé Charles Batteux, *Les Beaux-Arts réduits à un seul principe* (Paris, 1747).

4. Jean B. de Laborde, *Essai sur la musique ancienne et moderne* (Paris, 1780–1781), I, 394.

5. Jean Jacques Rousseau, *Lettre sur la musique française* (Paris, 1753).

6. Friedrich Melchior Grimm, *Le Petit Prophète de Boehmischbroda* (1753), in Henri de Curzon, *La Musique* (Paris, 1914), p. 175.

7. Denis Diderot, *Second Entretien* to *Le Fils naturel* (1757), in F. C. Green, *Diderot's Writings on the Theater* (Cambridge, 1936), p. 51.

8. For analysis of these librettos see Guiet, *op. cit.*, pp. 43 f.

9. Charles Perrault, *Parallèle des anciens et des modernes* (Paris, 1692), in *Œuvres*, III, 283–284.

10. Jean François Marmontel, *Eléments de la littérature* (Paris, 1777), article on "Opéra."

11. Jean F. Saint-Lambert, Marquis de, *Lettre à M. le B. . . . d'H. . . .* [Baron d'Holbach] *sur l'opéra*, in François Arnaud, *Variétés Littéraires* (Paris, 1768–1769), IV, 4.

12. Pierre J. B. Nougaret, *De l'art du théâtre en général* (Paris, 1769), II, 214.

13. Eugène Briffault, "L'Opéra," *Paris ou le Livre des Cent-et-Un* (Brussels, 1835), XV, 360.

14. Gustave Chouquet, *Histoire de la musique dramatique en France* (Paris, 1873), p. 383.

15. Jean T. Merle, *De l'Opéra* (Paris, 1827), pp. 21–22.

16. Letter from Meyerbeer to Dr. Schucht in 1852, quoted in Henri Blaze de Bury, *Meyerbeer et son temps* (Paris, 1865), pp. 245–246.

17. Louis Véron, *Mémoires d'un bourgeois de Paris* (Paris, 1856–1857), III, 61.

18. Albert Le Roy, *L'Aube du théâtre romantique* (Paris, 1904), p. 23.

19. Adolphe Jullien, *Paris dilettante au commencement du siècle* (Paris, 1884), pp. 306–307.

20. Alfred de Musset, *La Confession d'un enfant du siècle* in *Œuvres Complètes* (Paris, 1876), Vol. VIII, Ch. ii, p. 6.

21. Hippolyte Parigot, *Alexandre Dumas père* (Paris, 1902), p. 54.

22. James F. Mason, *The Melodrama in France from the Revolution to the Beginning of the Romantic Drama* (Baltimore, 1912), p. 172.

23. Frederick W. M. Draper, *The Rise and Fall of the French Romantic Drama* (London, 1923), p. 15.

24. See Mme. de Staël, *De l'Allemagne* (1810), Vol. II, Ch. xv; and Stendhal, *Racine et Shakespeare* (1823).

25. Hippolyte A. Taine, *Histoire de la littérature anglaise* (second edition, Paris, 1905), IV, 277.

26. Mason, *op. cit.*, p. 179.

27. Hippolyte Parigot, *Le Drame d'Alexandre Dumas* (Paris, 1898), p. 182.

28. Lamartine, *Des Destinées de la poésie*, "Les Grands Ecrivains de la France," edited Gustave Lanson (Paris, 1915), p. 413.

29. Parigot, *Le Théâtre d'hier* (Paris, 1893), p. x.

30. N. H. Clement, *Romanticism in France* (New York, 1939), p. 442.

31. *La Muette,* Act IV.

32. *Gustave III,* Act I.

33. Jullien, *op. cit.*, p. 306.

34. *Guillaume Tell*, Act I.

35. *Guillaume Tell*, Act II.

36. *La Juive*, Act III.

37. *Les Huguenots*, Act II.

38. Théophile Gautier, *Histoire de l'art dramatique en France* (Paris, 1858), V, 289.

39. Castil-Blaze, *De l'opéra en France* (Paris, 1820), I, 71.

40. Notable exceptions occur in *La Juive* where the second act ends with a trio and the fourth act with a solo; and in *Les Huguenots* where the famous duet between Raoul and Valentine brings Act Four to a close.

41. Gautier, *op. cit.*, VI, 52.

CHAPTER 8

1. Alfred A. Ernouf, *L'Art musical au XIXe siècle* (Paris, 1888), p. 154.

2. Henri Eymieu, *L'Œuvre de Meyerbeer* (Paris, 1910), p. 11.

3. Letter dated Milan, July 5, 1823; quoted in Henri Blaze de Bury, *Meyerbeer et son temps* (Paris, 1865), p. 51.

4. Lionel Dauriac, *Meyerbeer* (Paris, 1930), p. 30.

5. *La Revue Musicale*, II (1828), 424.

6. Castil-Blaze, *L'Académie Impériale de Musique* (Paris, 1855), II, 126.

7. Sophie Leo, "Musical Life in Paris (1817–1848)," *The Musical Quarterly*, XVII (1931), 262.

8. "Opera in Paris during the Last Thirty Years (1820–1850)," *Bentley's Miscellany*, September, 1851, p. 231.

9. Castil-Blaze, *op. cit.*, II, 178.

10. *Ibid.*, II, 181.

11. Hector Berlioz, *Mémoires* (Paris, 1878), I, 83.

12. Jacques F. Halévy, *Derniers souvenirs et portraits* (Paris, 1863), p. 146.

13. *La Revue Musicale*, I (1828), 186.

14. Théophile Gautier, *Histoire de l'art dramatique en France* (Paris, 1858), I, 44.

15. *Le Globe*, August 5, 1829.

16. Gautier, *La Musique* (Paris, 1911), p. 125.

17. Francis Toye, *Rossini: A Study in Tragi-comedy* (London, 1934), p. 252.

18. Gautier, *Histoire de l'art dramatique en France*, I, 339.

19. *Ibid.*, I, 85.

20. In two letters written shortly before his death Rossini argued that "pleasure must be the foundation and the aim of musical art,"

and recommended that young composers should strive to create simple, clear melody, avoiding any traffic with "the new esthetic principles which would transform music into a literary art or a philosophical melopœia." Quoted in *Encyclopédie de la musique et dictionnaire du Conservatoire* (Paris, 1920–1931), Part I, III, 855.

21. Louis M. Quicherat, *Adolphe Nourrit* (Paris, 1867), I, 144.

22. Hector Berlioz, *Mémoires* (Paris, 1878), II, 346.

23. See *La Juive:* Act I, Leopold's serenade, "Si la rigueur." Act II, Eléazar's cavatina, "Dieu! que ma voix tremblante." Act III, Eudora's air, "Tandis qu'il sommeille." Act IV, Eléazar's air, "Rachel, quand du seigneur."

24. Lionel de la Laurencie, *Lully* (Paris, 1919), p. 144.

25. This is true also in Beethoven's *Fidelio* (1805).

26. Jean T. Merle, *De l'Opéra* (Paris, 1827), p. 35.

27. Edouard Schuré, *Le Drame musical* (Paris, 1886), I, 253.

28. A particularly effective use of the unison chorus occurs in the third act of Auber's *Gustave III,* where the conspirators sing pianissimo the mocking words:

> Admirable conquête!
>
> Quoi! ces époux heureux,
>
> Tous deux, en tête-à-tête
>
> Se trouvaient en ces lieux!

29. Camille Saint-Saëns, *Ecole Buissonnière* (Paris, 1913), p. 280.

30. Louis Véron, *Mémoires d'un bourgeois de Paris* (Paris, 1856–1857), III, 162.

31. See Hector Berlioz, *Grand traité d'instrumentation et d'orchestration* (Paris, 1844); also Henri Lavoix, *Histoire de l'instrumentation depuis le seizième siècle* (Paris, 1878).

32. See Herman Kretzschmar, "Die musikgeschichtliche Bedeutung Simon Mayrs," *Jahrbuch Peters* (Leipzig, 1904); also Ludwig Schiedermair, *Simon Mayr* (Leipzig, 1907).

33. *La Revue Musicale,* I (1827), 83.

34. See Lavoix, *op. cit.,* pp. 372 ff.; and Toye, *op. cit.*

35. Stendhal, *Memoirs of Rossini* (London, 1824), p. 269.

36. Ludovic Vitet, *Etudes sur les beaux-arts* (Paris, 1846), I, 64.

37. Alfred de Musset, "Concert de Mademoiselle Garcia," *La Revue des Deux Mondes,* XVII (January 1, 1839), p. 113.

38. Henri M. Berton, *De la musique mécanique et de la musique philosophique* (Paris, 1826), p. 34.

39. Heinrich Heine, *Über die französische Bühne, Vertraute Briefe an August Lewald,* Vol. VI of *Sämtliche Werke* (Munich, 1925), 9th Letter.

40. Henri Blaze de Bury, *Meyerbeer et son temps* (Paris, 1865), p. 73.

41. Robert Schumann, *Music and Musicians,* translated by F. R. Richter (first series, fifth edition, London, 1877), p. 302.

42. Felix Mendelssohn-Bartholdy, *Letters of Felix Mendelssohn-Bartholdy from Italy and Switzerland,* translated by Lady Wallace (New York, 1869), p. 325.

43. Richard Wagner, *Opera and Drama,* translated by W. A. Ellis (London, 1892–1899), II, 95.

44. *Le Moniteur universel,* November 24, 1831.

45. George Sand, *Lettres d'un voyageur, Œuvres* (Paris, 1847), IX, 347.

46. Honoré Balzac, *Gambara,* Vol. IX, *La Comédie humaine* (Paris, 1937), p. 462.

47. Hector Berlioz, *Mémoires* (Paris, 1878), II, 108.

48. Excerpt from an unprinted article written by Wagner in 1842; quoted in Albert Soubies and Charles Malherbe, *Mélanges sur Richard Wagner* (Paris, 1892), p. 123.

49. See the excellent essay on Meyerbeer in Bernard van Dieren, *Down Among the Dead Men* (London, 1935).

CHAPTER 9

1. Louis Véron, *Mémoires d'un bourgeois de Paris* (Paris, 1856–1857), III, 181–182.

2. Richard Wagner, *Opera and Drama,* translated by W. A. Ellis (London, 1892–1899), II, 29–30.

3. Alfred de Musset, "Concert de Mademoiselle Garcia," *Revue des Deux Mondes,* XVII, January 1, 1839, 112–113.

4. Joseph L. d'Ortigue, *Le Balcon de l'Opéra* (Paris, 1833), p. 164.

5. Wagner, *op. cit.,* II, 29.

6. Jean de La Bruyère, *Les Caractères* (Paris, 1932), Ch. I, "Des Ouvrages de l'Esprit," p. 79.

7. Emile Deschamps, *Lettres sur la musique,* Vol. IV of *Œuvres complètes* (Paris, 1873), pp. 27–28.

BIBLIOGRAPHY

Abraham, Gerald E. H. A Hundred Years of Music. London, 1938.
Adam, Adolphe C. Derniers souvenirs d'un musicien. Paris, 1871.
———— Souvenirs d'un musicien. Paris, 1859.
Allévy, Marie Antoinette. La Mise en Scène en France dans la pre-
    mière moitié du dix-neuvième siècle. Paris, 1938.
Altmann, W. "Meyerbeer-Forschungen." Sammelbände der Inter-
    nationalen Musikgesellschaft, IV, 1902–1903.
d'Alton-Shée, Comte Edmond. Mes Mémoires (1826–1848). Paris,
    1869.
Arrigon, Louis J. Les Années romantiques de Balzac. Paris, 1927.
Artz, Frederick B. France under the Bourbon Restoration (1814–
    1830). Cambridge, 1931.
———— Reaction and Revolution (1814–1832). New York, 1934.
Arvin, Neil C. Eugène Scribe and the French Theater. Cambridge,
    1924.
Barzun, Jacques. Darwin, Marx, Wagner. Boston, 1941.
———— Romanticism and the Modern Ego. Boston, 1943.
Beauquier, Charles. La Musique et le drame. Paris, 1877.
Bekker, Paul. The Changing Opera. New York, 1935.
———— The Story of the Orchestra. New York, 1936.
Bennett, Joseph. Giacomo Meyerbeer. London (188–?).
Berlioz, Hector. Grand Traité d'instrumentation et d'orchestration.
    Paris, 1844.
———— Mémoires. Paris, 1878.
Berton, Henri M. De la Musique mécanique et de la musique
    philosophique. Paris, 1826.

Bertrand, Gustave. Les Nationalités musicales étudiées dans le drame lyrique. Paris, 1872.

Beyle, Marie Henri. Vie de Rossini. Edited by Henri Prunières, Paris, 1922.

Bie, Oscar. Die Oper. Berlin, 1923.

Blaze de Bury, Henri. Meyerbeer et son temps. Paris, 1865.

———— Musiciens contemporains. Paris, 1856.

Boigne, Charles de. Petits mémoires de l'Opéra. Paris, 1857.

Bonald, Louis G. A. de. Mélanges. 3rd ed., Paris, 1852.

Bonnefon, Paul. "Scribe sous la Monarchie de Juillet, d'après des Documents Inédits." *Revue d'Histoire Littéraire de la France,* January–April, 1921.

Boschot, Adolphe. Chez les musiciens. 3rd series, 6th ed., Paris, 1926.

Bossuet, Pierre. Histoire administrative des rapports des théâtres et de l'Etat. Paris, 1909.

Bouchot, Henri. Le Luxe français: La Restauration. Paris, 1893.

Boulenger, Jacques. Les Dandys. Paris, 1932.

Bouteron, Marcel. Danse et musique romantiques. Paris, 1927.

Brandes, George. Main Currents in Nineteenth-Century Literature. New York, 1923.

Bricqueville, E. de. Le Livret d'opéra français de Lully à Gluck. Paris, 1887.

Briffault, Eugène. "L'Opéra." *Paris ou le Livre des Cent-et-Un.* Brussels, 1835, XV.

Brunetière, Ferdinand. Manuel de l'histoire de la littérature française. Paris, 1899.

Bücken, Ernst. "Musik des 19. Jahrhunderts bis zur Moderne." *Handbuch der Musikwissenschaft,* Leipzig, 1928–1934, VI.

Bureau, Georges. Le Théâtre et sa législation. Paris, 1898.

Carr, Philip. Days with the French Romantics. London, 1932.

Castil-Blaze (François Henri J. Blaze). De l'opéra en France. Paris, 1820.

———— L'Académie Impériale de Musique. Paris, 1855.

———— Mémorial du Grand Opéra. Paris, 1847.

———— Sur l'opéra français: Vérités dures mais utiles. Paris, 1856.

Castille, Hippolyte. "Les Hommes et les Mœurs sous le Règne de Louis-Philippe." *Revue de Paris,* July–August, 1853.

Ces Demoiselles de l'Opéra. Paris, 1887.

Challamel, Jean B. Album de l'Opéra. Paris, 1845.

Chasles, Philarète. Mémoires. Paris, 1877.

Chorley, Henry F. Music and Manners in France and Germany. London, 1844.

———— Thirty Years' Musical Recollections. London, 1862.

Choron, Alexandre E. and Fayolle, F. J. M. Dictionnaire historique des musiciens, artistes et amateurs. Paris, 1810–1811.

Chouquet, Gustave. Histoire de la musique dramatique en France. Paris, 1873.

Clement, N. H. Romanticism in France. "Revolving Fund Series," IX, of The Modern Language Association of America; New York, 1939.

Combarieu, Jules. "Meyerbeer." *Revue d'Histoire et de Critique Musicale*, Paris, IV, 1904.

Crozet, F. Revue de la musique dramatique en France. Paris, 1866.

Curzon, Henri de. "Les Grands Succès de l'Opéra de 1673 à 1825 et ce qu'il en reste." *Revue Internationale de Musique*, February, 1899.

———— Meyerbeer. "Les Musiciens Célèbres"; Paris, 1910.

Daguerre, Louis J. M. Historique et Description des Procédés du Daguerréotype et du Diorama. Paris, 1839.

Dandelot, Arthur. Evolution de la musique de théâtre depuis Meyerbeer jusqu'à nos jours. Paris, 1927.

Dauriac, Lionel. La Psychologie dans l'opéra français. Paris, 1897.

———— Meyerbeer. Paris, 1930.

Delécluze, Etienne. Souvenirs de soixante années. Paris, 1862.

Deschamps, Emile. Lettres sur la musique. Œuvres complètes, IV. Paris, 1873.

Deshayes, A. J. J. Idées générales sur l'Académie Royale. Paris, 1822.

Destranges, Etienne. L'Œuvre théâtrale de Meyerbeer. Paris, 1893.

Diderot, Denis. De la Poésie dramatique. Œuvres complètes, VII, Paris, 1875.

Doumic, René. De Scribe à Ibsen. Paris, 1896.

———— Hommes et idées du XIXᵉ siècle. Paris, 1903.

Draper, Frederick W. M. The Rise and Fall of the French Romantic Drama. London, 1923.

Du Camp, Maxime. Souvenirs littéraires. Paris, 1892.

Du Fayl, Ezvar. Académie Nationale de Musique, 1671–1877. Paris, 1878.

Dumas, Alexandre. Souvenirs dramatiques. Paris, 1881.

———— Théâtre complet. Paris, 1864.

Ecorcheville, J. De Lully à Rameau, l'esthétique musicale. Paris, 1906.

Edwards, Henry S. The Lyrical Drama. London, 1881.

Ehrhard, Auguste. "L'Opéra sous la Direction Véron." *Revue Musicale de Lyon*, V, 1907.

———— Une Vie de danseuse: Fanny Elssler. Paris, 1909.

Encyclopédie de la musique et dictionnaire du Conservatoire. Paris, 1920–1931.

Ernouf, Alfred A. L'Art musical au XIXᵉ siècle. Paris, 1888.

Evans, David-Owen. Le Drame moderne à l'époque romantique (1827–1850). Paris, 1923.

———— Les Problemes d'actualité au théâtre à l'époque romantique (1827–1850). Paris, 1923.

———— Le Théâtre pendant la période romantique (1827–1848). Paris, 1925.

Evans, Raymond L. Les Romantiques français et la musique. Paris, 1934.

Eymieu, Henri. L'Œuvre de Meyerbeer. Paris, 1910.

Fischer, Carlos. Les Costumes de l'Opéra. Paris, 1931.

Gautier, Théophile. Histoire de l'art dramatique en France. Paris, 1858.

———— Histoire du Romantisme. 2nd ed., Paris, 1874.

———— La Musique. Paris, 1911.

———— Les Beautés de l'Opéra. Paris, 1845.

———— Portraits contemporains. 3rd ed., Paris, 1874.

———— Souvenirs de théâtre, d'art et de critique. Paris, 1883.

Geoffroy, Julien L. Cours de littérature dramatique. 2nd ed., Paris, 1825.

Girard, Henri. Un Bourgeois dilettante à l'époque romantique: Emile Deschamps. Paris, 1921.

Girardin, Madame Emile de. Lettres Parisiennes. Paris, 1868.

Green, F. C. Diderot's Writings on the Theater. Cambridge, 1936.

Grétry, Andre E. M. Mémoires ou essais sur la musique. Paris, 1797.

Gros, Etienne. Philippe Quinault, sa vie et son œuvre. Paris, 1925.

Guex, Jules. Le Théâtre et la société française de 1815 à 1848. Paris, 1900.

Guiet, René. L'Evolution d'un genre: Le Livret d'opéra en France de Gluck à la révolution (1774–1793), "Smith College Studies in Modern Languages," XVIII; Northampton, 1936–1937.

Guilbert de Pixérécourt, Réné Charles. "Le Mélodrame." *Paris ou le Livre des Cent-et-Un*, Paris, 1832, VI.

———— "Derniers Réflexions de l'Auteur sur le Mélodrame." In Pixérécourt, Théâtre choisi, IV. Nancy, 1843.

Halévy, Jacques Fromentin. Derniers souvenirs et portraits. Paris, 1863.

———— Souvenirs et portraits. Paris, 1861.

Halévy, Leon. F. Halévy, sa vie et ses œuvres. Paris, 1863.

Hautecœur, Louis. Le Romantisme et l'art. Paris, 1928.

Heine, Heinrich. Über die französische Bühne, Vertraute Briefe an August Lewald, Vol. VI of Sämtliche Werke, edited by Fritz Strich. Munich, 1925.

Hennin, Michel. Des Théâtres et de leur organisation légale. Paris, 1819.

Hermann, Jacques. Le Drame lyrique en France depuis Gluck jusqu'à nos jours. Paris, 1878.

Hervey, Arthur. French Music of the Nineteenth Century. London, 1903.

Hogarth, George. Memoirs of the Musical Drama. London, 1838.

Holsboer, S. Wilma. Histoire de la mise en scène dans le théâtre français de 1600 à 1657. Paris, 1933.

Houssaye, Arsène. Les Confessions; Souvenirs d'un demi-siècle, 1830–1880. Paris, 1885.

———— Princesses de comédie et déesses d'opéra. Paris, 1860.

Hugo, Victor. Œuvres complètes. Paris, 1912.

Istel, Edgar. Das Buch der Oper. Berlin, 1919.

Janin, Jules. Histoire de la littérature dramatique. Paris, 1854.

Janin, Jules and Chasles, Philarète. Les Beautés de l'Opéra. Paris, 1845.

Jullien, Adolphe. Musique; Mélanges d'histoire et de critique musicale et dramatique. Paris, 1896.

———— Paris dilettante au commencement du siècle. Paris, 1884.

Kretzschmar, Hermann. Geschichte der Oper. Leipzig, 1919.

———— "Die Musikgeschichtliche Bedeutung Simon Mayrs." *Jahrbuch Peters*, XI, 1904.

La Borde, Jean B. de. Essai sur la musique ancienne et moderne. Paris, 1780–1781.

Lacey, Alexander. Pixérécourt and the French Romantic Drama. Toronto, 1928.

Lacroix, Paul. Directoire, Consulat et Empire, 1795–1815. 2nd ed., Paris, 1885.

Lajarte, Théodore de. Curiosités de l'Opéra. Paris, 1883.

La Laurencie, Lionel de. Histoire du goût musical en France. Paris, 1905.

———— Les Créateurs de l'opéra français. Paris, 1930.

———— "Les Idées de Stendhal sur la Musique." *La Revue Musicale*, December 1924.

———— Lully. Paris, 1919.

Lamartine, Alphonse de. Des Destinées de la poésie. "Les Grands Ecrivains de la France," edited by Gustave Lanson; Paris, 1915.

Láng, Paul H. Music in Western Civilization. New York, 1941.

Lasalle, Albert de. Les Treize Salles de l'opéra. Paris, 1875.

———— Meyerbeer; Sa Vie et le catalogue de ses œuvres. Paris, 1864.

Lasserre, Pierre. The Spirit of French Music. Translated by Denis Turner, New York, 1921.

Lavoix, Henri. Histoire de l'instrumentation depuis le seizième siècle. Paris, 1878.

Le Breton, André. Le Théâtre romantique. Paris (1927?).

Legouvé, Ernest. Eugène Scribe. Paris, 1874.

Leo, Sophie Augustine. "Musical Life in Paris (1817–1848)," a chapter from Erinnerungen aus Paris. Berlin, 1851, translated by Oliver Strunk, *Musical Quarterly*, XVII, 1931.

Le Roy, Albert. L'Aube du théâtre romantique. Paris, 1904.

Leveaux, Alphonse. Nos Théâtres de 1800 à 1880. Paris, 1881–1886.

Levinson, André. Marie Taglioni (1804–1884). Paris, 1929.

Locke, Arthur W. Music and the Romantic Period in France. London, 1920.

Loustalan, Henri A. B. La Publicité dans la presse française. Paris, 1933.

Lucas-Dubreton, Jean. The Restoration and the July Monarchy, Vol. VIII of The National History of France. 1929.

———— La Royauté Bourgeoise. Paris, 1930.

The Lyric Drama. Extracted from the *British and Foreign Review or European Quarterly Journal*, No. XXIII, London, 1841.

Maigron, Louis. Le Romantisme et la mode. Paris, 1911.

Marmontel, Antoine F. Eléments d'esthétique musicale et considérations sur le beau dans les arts. Paris, 1846.

———— Essai sur les révolutions de la musique en France. Paris, 1777.

Marsan, Jules. La Bataille romantique. Paris, 1912.

Martine, J. D. De la musique dramatique en France. Paris, 1813.

Mason, James F. The Melodrama in France from the Revolution to the Beginning of Romantic Drama. Baltimore, 1912.

Masson, Paul M. L'Opéra de Rameau. Paris, 1930.

Matthews, Brander. A Book about the Theater. New York, 1916.

———— French Dramatists of the Nineteenth Century. New York, 1901.

Maurice, Charles. Histoire Anecdotique du Théâtre. Paris, 1856.

Mendelssohn-Bartholdy, Felix. Letters of Felix Mendelssohn-Bartholdy from Italy and Switzerland, translated by Lady Wallace. New York, 1869.

Merle, Jean T. Du Marasme dramatique en 1829. Paris, 1829.

———— De l'Opéra. Paris, 1827.

Moscheles, Felix. Letters of Felix Mendelssohn to Ignaz and Charlotte Moscheles, translated by Felix Moscheles. London, 1888.

Nerval, Gérard de. Notes d'un amateur de musique. Intro. by André Cœuroy, Paris, 1926.

Nicoll, Allardyce. The Development of the Theater. Revised edition, London, 1937.

Noel, E. Les Annales du théâtre et de la musique. Paris, 1858.

Nougaret, Pierre J. B. De l'art du théâtre en général. Paris, 1769.

"Opera in Paris during the Last Thirty Years (1820–1850)," *Bentley's Miscellany*. London, September, 1851.

d'Ortigue, Joseph L. De la guerre des dilettanti, ou de la révolution opérée par Rossini dans l'opéra français. Paris, 1830.

———— Du Théâtre-Italien et de son influence sur le goût musical français. Paris, 1840.

———— Le Balcon de l'Opéra. Paris, 1833.

Parigot, Hippolyte. Alexandre Dumas père. Paris, 1902.

———— Le Drame d'Alexandre Dumas. Paris, 1898.

———— Le Théâtre d'hier. Paris, 1893.

Pelissier, Paul. Histoire administrative de l'Académie Nationale de Musique et de Danse. Paris, 1906.

Perrin, Emile. "Etude sur la Mise en Scène," *Les Annales du Théâtre et de la Musique*, 8th Année, 1882; Paris, 1883.

Pezzer, Raymond de. L'Opéra devant la loi et la jurisprudence. Paris, 1911.

Planche, Gustave. "Histoire et Philosophie de l'Art," *Revue des Deux Mondes,* IV, 1834.

Pougin, Arthur. F. Halévy: Ecrivain. Paris, 1865.

———— Le Théâtre à l'Exposition de 1889. Paris, 1890.

———— "Personnel et Repertoire de l'Opéra de 1821 à 1873," *Chronique Musicale*, Vol. II, No. 10. November 15, 1873.

———— Question de la liberté des théâtres. Paris, 1878.

Prod'homme, Jacques G. L'Opéra (1669–1925). Paris, 1925.

Quicherat, Louis M. Adolphe Nourrit. Paris, 1867.

Regnard, Albert. La Renaissance du drame lyrique 1600–1876. Paris, 1895.

Rew, Cecil Lewis. Literary Theories of the French Romanticists. Urbana, 1935.

Rosenthal, Leon. L'Art et les artistes romantiques. Paris, 1928.

Royer, Alphonse. Histoire de l'Opéra. Paris, 1875.

Saint-Saëns, Camille. Ecole Buissonnière. Paris, 1913.

Sand, George. Lettres d'un voyageur. Paris, 1843.

Schemann, L. L. Cherubini. Stuttgart, 1925.

Schiedermair, Ludwig. Beitrage zur Geschichte der Oper um die Wende des 18. und 19. Jahrhunderts. Leipzig, 1907–1910.

———— Simon Mayr. Leipzig, 1907.

Schumann, Robert. Music and Musicians. 1st series, translated by F. R. Richter, 5th edition, London, 1877 (?).

Schuré, Edouard. Le Drame musical. Paris, 1886.

Scribe, Eugène. Œuvres complètes. Paris, 1899.

Scudo, Paul. Critique et littérature musicales. Paris, 1856.

———— De l'influence du mouvement romantique sur l'art musical et du rôle qu'a voulu jouer M. H. Berlioz. Paris, 1846.

———— L'Année musicale. Paris, 1860.

———— L'Art ancien et l'art moderne. Paris, 1854.

Séchan, Charles P. Souvenirs d'un homme de théâtre, 1831–1855. Paris, 1883.

Servières, G. Episodes d'histoire musicale. Paris, 1914.

———— "La Première Représentation de *Guillaume Tell* à Paris," *Rivista Musicale Italiana*, XXXVI, 1929.

Soubies, Albert. Le Théâtre-Italien de 1801 à 1913. Paris, 1913.

———— Soixante Ans à l'Opéra du *Siège de Corinthe* à la *Walkyrie* (1826–1893). Paris, 1893.

Soubies, Albert and Malherbe, Charles. Mélanges sur Richard Wagner. Paris, 1892.

"Symposium on Romanticism," *Journal of the History of Ideas,* II, June 1941.

Tiersot, Jullien. Hector Berlioz et la société de son temps. Paris, 1904.
——— "Music and the Centenary of Romanticism." *Musical Quarterly*, XV, 1929.
Toye, Francis. Rossini: A Study in Tragi-Comedy. London, 1934.
Treille, M. Le Conflit dramatique en France de 1823 à 1830 d'après les journaux du temps. Paris, 1929.
Van Dieren, Bernard. Down Among the Dead Men, and Other Essays. London, 1935.
Van Tieghem, Paul. Le Mouvement romantique (Angleterre—Allemagne—Italie—France). 2nd ed., Paris, 1923.
Véron, Louis. Mémoires d'un bourgeois de Paris, 1856–1857.
Viel-Castel, Horace, Comte de. Mémoires. Paris, 1883.
Vitet, Ludovic. Etudes sur les beaux-arts. Paris, 1846.
Wagner, Richard. Prose Works. Translated by W. A. Ellis. London, 1892–1899.
Wright, C. H. Conrad. A History of French Literature. New York, 1912.

INDEX

Libretto, in classical French opera, 83 f.; reforms of Zeno and Metastasio, 84; in 18th century French opera, 84 f.; halts on outskirts of Romanticism, 88; revolution effected by Scribe, 89 f.; historical material in, 92 f.; treatment of love in, 97 f.; language of, 100; dramatic design of, 100 f.

Lodoiska, Cherubini, 87
Louis IX en Egypte, Le Moyne, 86
Louis XI, Delavigne, 75
Louis XIV, 11, 132
Louis XVIII, 8, 14, 109
Louis-Philippe, 4, 10, 17, 20, 24, 29, 106
Lubbert, 14, 15, 19, 20
Lully, 1, 4, 11, 32-33, 36, 51, 52, 80, 84, 89, 118, 124, 127, 132

Maistre, Joseph de, 39
Malibran, Marie, 40
Malitourne, 23
Marino Faliero, Delavigne, 75
Marmontel, 86
Marriage of Figaro, Mozart, 110
Masaniello, Moreau and Lafortelle, 89
Massimilla Doni, Balzac, 78
Maurice, Charles, 25
Mayr, Johann Simon, 6, 125, 126
Mazarin, Cardinal, 36, 51
Méhul, 87, 108, 119
Melodrama, 54 f., 92
Mendelssohn, 127
Mérimée, Prosper, 78, 90, 93
Merll, J. T., 88
Messager des Chambres, periodical, 22
Metastasio, Pietro, 80
Metropolitan Opera House, 43
Meyerbeer, 1, 2, 3, 5, 6, 35, 38, 40, 41, 47, 61, 69, 78, 90, 106, 113-117, 121-129, 131, 132
   Abimelech, 106
   Emma di Resburgo, 107
   Crociato, Il, 107, 127
   Jepthas Gelübde, 106
   Les Huguenots, 1, 39, 45, 72, 74,

89-90, 93, 95, 96, 101, 103, 104, 112, 116, 120, 125, 127, 128
   Margherita d'Angiù, 38, 107
   Robert le Diable, 2, 3, 38, 40, 47, 61-63, 78, 89, 91, 98, 99, 101, 103, 104, 107, 113-117, 120, 121, 126, 127, 128
   Romilde e Constanza, 107
   Semiramide riconosciuta, 107
Michelet, 93
Middle Ages, representation at Opéra, 62 f., 88; public interest in, 92
Miltiade à Marathon, Le Moyne, 87
Misanthrope, Le, Molière, 89
Mise en scène, in classic French opera, 51 f.; in classic French drama, 52; trend toward realism in 18th century, 52 f.; in melodrama, 54 f.; in romantic theater, 56 f.; at Opéra in early 19th century, 58; modernization by Duponchel and Cicéri, 58 f.; lavishness criticized, 66 f.; influence on drama and music, 69, 105
Molière, 76
Moniteur Universel, periodical, 128
Monsigny, 71, 109
Montalivet, Comte de, 19
Montguyon, Comte Fernand de, 31
Mort d'Adam et son Apothéose, Le Sueur, 88
Mort du Tasse, La, Garcia, 108
Mozart, 48, 110, 113, 119, 130
Musard, 30
Music at Opéra (see aria, characterization, chorus, orchestra), prior to Meyerbeer's appearance, 1811-1831, 108 f.; reformed by Rossini, 11 f.; influence of *La Muette*, 112; influence of *Guillaume Tell*, 113 f.; Meyerbeer takes leadership, 113 f.; formal design of grand opera, 121 f.; search for grandiose, 123 f.; shaped to character of stage, 128
Musset, Alfred de, 78, 92, 111, 126, 130

Napoleon, 8, 9, 56, 88, 92, 111
Natalie, Reicha, 108

VITA

William Loran Crosten was born in Des Moines, Iowa, September 7, 1909. He received the degrees of Bachelor of Music from Drake University in 1930, Master of Arts from the University of Iowa in 1936, and Doctor of Philosophy from Columbia University in 1946. While at Columbia he held the Mosenthal Fellowship (1938), the Lydia Roberts Fellowship (1939), and the Clarence Barker Fellowship (1940). He is now associate professor of music and executive head of the Department of Music at Stanford University.

A section from this book, "Auguste and His Claque," has been previously published as an article in the *Musical Quarterly* (April, 1946).